THERE IS HOPE

THE SHAWN MOORE STORY

SHAWN MOORE

There is Hope The Shawn Moore Story

Printed in the United States of America

Paperback ISBN: 9798329731095

Editing: Rine, C. Rebecca

Cover Design: Ears to hear, Chavos Buycks

Purpose Publishing LLC.
13194 US Highway 301 South
Suite 417
Riverview, Florida 33578

www.PurposePublishing.com

To Jennifer, the one who typed every word of this book. Thank you.

Special thanks to God for what He has done with my life.

TABLE OF CONTENTS

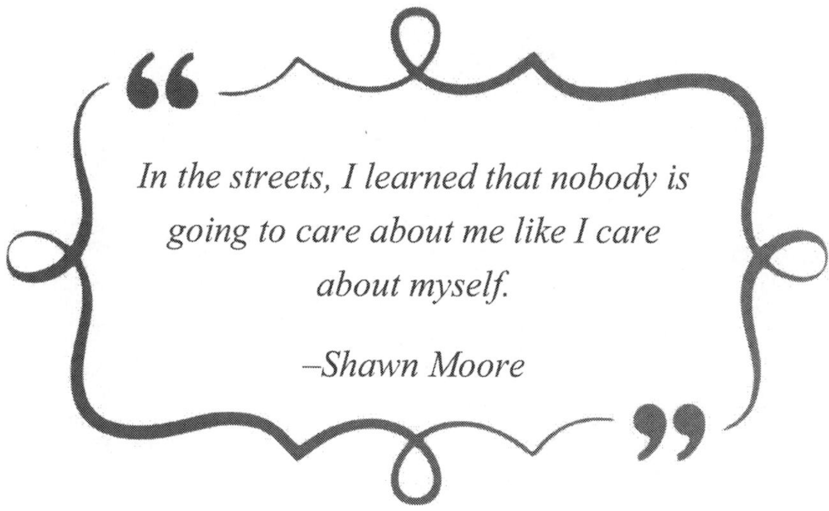
In the streets, I learned that nobody is going to care about me like I care about myself.

–Shawn Moore

INTRODUCTION

It's 2020, and my name is Shawn Moore. I am currently involved in four mentorship programs. I am guilty of spending countless hours a week in four different elementary schools trying to make a difference in some young person's life. Exposure is so important to young people who find it hard to dream. I have been privileged to do some one-on-one mentoring as well as have the opportunity to speak to groups of young people—sometimes more than fifty kids at once. It breaks my heart to hear some of their stories and realize from their behavior and attitude where most of them are headed.

I haven't always been a senseless violence activist, author, mentor, and man of God. I had my fair share of making unwise decisions. I could have been LOCKED UP! SENT DOWN THE RIVER, INCARCERATED, jailed, doin' time…

I hope by me sharing some of my story people don't define me by the bad decisions I made in life. I have learned from those bad decisions and have changed. That is why I am writing this book and why I hope you will learn something from reading it.

So many young men have lost their freedom, and even more have lost their lives. I know it looks like there is no hope at all with everybody having a gun and no one caring whether they live or die. I get it. I have lost a lot of friends to the streets. They either went to prison or died at a young age by the hands of gun violence. But because of how my life has turned out, I believe in hope now. Whereas before I didn't. What advice would you give someone like me who was or is headed in the direction of imprisonment?

Hopefully, you will tell them about Shawn Moore. I was guilty of taking the circuitous route to maturity, like so many young people today. I didn't decide to do something with my life until I was twenty-eight years old. I am highly qualified to talk about change in the streets because Shawn Moore was a street person who has changed. My goal in writing this book is to push others to think futuristically and not to just live in the moment or the here and now.

This statement is important, so keep it in your mind as you read my story. The only reason my life has turned out the way it did compared to millions of others is my decision to believe in God and live for God at the young age of nine years old. My family and I stayed in church, and I believed in God and wanted to obey and live for Him desperately. But I got caught up wanting to have friends so badly that I was willing to compromise my faith to fit in.

A person who doesn't have the wisdom of God is in trouble. I was taught right from wrong and the difference between truth and error at a young age. The information I knew helped me navigate in the streets a little differently without losing my mind, even though I was close at times. I was determined to be a part of the streets despite the risks.

My friends and I had heard plenty about the risks involved in the type of life we were living, but we just did not believe or did not care that those risks would catch up to us one day. Let me tell you now that we were so wrong. We became a part of violent crimes and the constant mishandling of guns, drugs, alcohol, sex, and the list goes on and on and on. Some of us were murdered, some became shooters, and I know some killers. Others got strung out on drugs, or became drunks and contracted STDs, or stayed in and out of jail and prison. It's a vicious cycle for many. They do their time and are released, only to be back in jail within a year or less. Life is not lived but merely survived, and the future seems hopeless.

Many young people don't have family or real friends who care enough to catch them when they fall. But God cares, and Shawn

Moore cares, if don't nobody else cares about people making unwise decisions.

Truthfully, I only care because it could have been me. It could have been my family. But by the grace of God and making better decisions, I am no longer hustling or waking up every day with violence or murder on my mind. I know that pain is passed down from generation to generation, but we must learn to pass down to others that life is all about learning. Therefore, since God took the time to "instruct me and teach me in the way which I was to go and to guide me," (Psalm 32:8, paraphrased), it's only right for me to try to impart what I have learned to others. Don't tell me that sharing a story isn't important. Stories have and will continue to touch and change lives.

I am fully aware the streets are way more dangerous today and that the kids are putting in way more work than we had to do when I was young. However, the struggle to survive and stay alive is still the same. The street life: I was there! I lived it!

One thing I learned over time is that if you are willing to make just a few small changes daily for the rest of your life, neither you nor your life will ever be the same. Life is filled with a myriad of choices that will dictate the course of the rest of our days. I was going down the wrong roads of life, making some dumb mistakes. Deep down, I knew I needed to make some changes. It's easy to believe that no one cares about you when, for the most part, that is true. We only have a few people in our lives who really care about us. However, not having a lot of people in our corner encouraging us to change is not an excuse to stay the same.

I want people in the streets to know if there was hope for me, then there is hope for everyone. I can't go to the grave without at least trying to make a difference, even if I only reach one person. That person needs to know: I care. God cares.

I went from living the street life to living an exemplary life. It sure isn't fair for me to live the life that I am living and not share my story. I hope my story may turn someone from day-to-day survival to really living. The life that I am living is not just for me.

I know we will not be able to bring an end to all of the violence, crime, and other problems of the world, because in our society today, ignorance and foolishness are becoming more acceptable than ever before.

Maybe you're reading this book because you know someone who needs to change. Maybe *you're* the one hoping to change.

No matter your circumstances, what do you think has to happen in a person's life for them to decide it's time to change?

It could be when someone is broke all the time, strung out on drugs, or a dipsomaniac. For me, it was when I realized that the life I was living wasn't taking me where I wanted to be.

Have you ever gone to the store to buy something and decided it cost too much, and you turned around and walked out of the store? Now, don't get it twisted: others were willing to pay that price. NOT me. And that is what got me in the end. I decided the street life cost too much.

Living the street life is going to cost you something eventually, and I've seen it firsthand: that cost will be expensive. Maybe you've already paid more than you wanted to—or watched someone else pay too much. Could be the loss of your freedom, your life, your reputation, or your peace. Someone may have killed one of your family members or friends. You may have injured or even killed an enemy, family member, or friend yourself. You may have destroyed your liver or kidneys by drinking too much. You may have sacrificed your money from having too many baby mommas, and now child support is catching up to you. Someone may have robbed you. Doing drugs affects your brain and your health. Get ready to lose some sleep, some peace from being anxious, paranoid, or just partying all night. You may lose your privacy because now you're in a cell with a Bunky continuously.

Living the street life will cost you something. I decided the cost was too much and decided to turn around and walk out the door of being a street person.

When I first started playing around with drugs, guns, and street people I didn't realize that I was really going to have to start killing people to keep living that lifestyle. But after a while, it became clear that everything wasn't up to me. I couldn't just jump in and jump out of this lifestyle whenever and however I wanted. The lifestyle had its own rules. And I certainly wasn't the rule-maker.

Many of us are born into messed-up environments. But just like playing spades, you must learn to play the cards you were dealt. Nobody comes out of their mother's womb a street person or a killer. The mindset of killing people is a learned behavior. Kids love to play together until they are taught differently.

What a colossal mistake to not be willing to learn from others! In the real world, prison doesn't look good on your resume. Many are refusing to listen, and it's costing them peace, joy, and financial and physical freedom when they get locked up or murdered way too young. I have friends who told me they cried in the shower in prison out of fear of someone seeing them crying. People are not happy in prison. Death is real and final. Being locked up isn't cool, nor should it be a badge of honor. Life is short, and there is no coming back from death.

If you visit the airport, White House, or police station and express thoughts of harming someone, the outcome would be unfavorable for you. Bad behavior starts with bad thoughts. No one has been murdered without someone thinking about it first. Many need to be challenged to start thinking differently. If I didn't change the way I was thinking, prison was in my future for sure. But I did not want to be one of those men spending time in prison because of being guilty of a black-on-black crime. I knew I had some issues when my thoughts were only to kill, destroy, finish, murder, annihilate, and terminate individuals' lives. I am so grateful that I realized I needed to change. I needed help with my attitude and anger.

It would be real nice if life gave us an opportunity to restart our day and let us make better choices after we have messed up, but life ain’t like that. Unfortunately, we must deal with the consequences of our choices for the rest of our lives. I am so grateful I started thinking about my choices before it was too late.

What about you? Are you making good or bad choices right now? What kind of person do you want to be? Start setting goals and get to work. That’s what I did. You reading this book is one of the goals I had.

In this book, I will tell you some of what I went through that led me to realize that I’d better change before I get locked up or ended up dead. I was finally willing to change at the age of twenty-eight, but only after having made a lot of mistakes and living through a lot of regrets and missed opportunities.

As I tell my story, I am not trying to paint a picture of me being tough, hard-core, or even perfect. I really don’t even believe in people being hard anymore, unless they don’t bleed. One day early in my life, I was having problems with this group of dudes, and I was afraid. My little cousin, who was in the streets more than I was, told me not to worry about them because they bleed just like everyone else. I didn’t fully understand what he meant by that statement until I got deeper into the game. No one is invincible. Everyone is vulnerable. Everyone bleeds. So it puzzles me how so many are talking, living, and acting like they can't be touched.

The purpose of sharing these stories with you is not to glorify the bad things I did. In fact, it’s the opposite. I want you to see how close I was to making a mistake that would have changed my life forever. And I want you to see how and why I justified my way of living before I decided to change. In the end, it was God who saved me and helped me walk on a better path.

I am a living testimony that change is possible no matter what choices you have made in the past. I am living proof that you do not have to be what you have always been or be like everyone else. You have a choice! In 1998, I made a choice that I was not going to continue to go down the same road that I had been on. To my surprise, I'm now living rather than merely surviving. This is my story—the Shawn Moore Story.

It's never too late to change, no matter what you have done. In chapter 1, I will show you how some *decisions* I made opened up the door for me to almost become a statistic.

The people in this book are real people, and all the stories are true, so for privacy as well as to avoid liability issues, I have substituted the names of my friends with the names of animals. But that is the only thing about this book that is made-up. Everything else couldn't be more real.

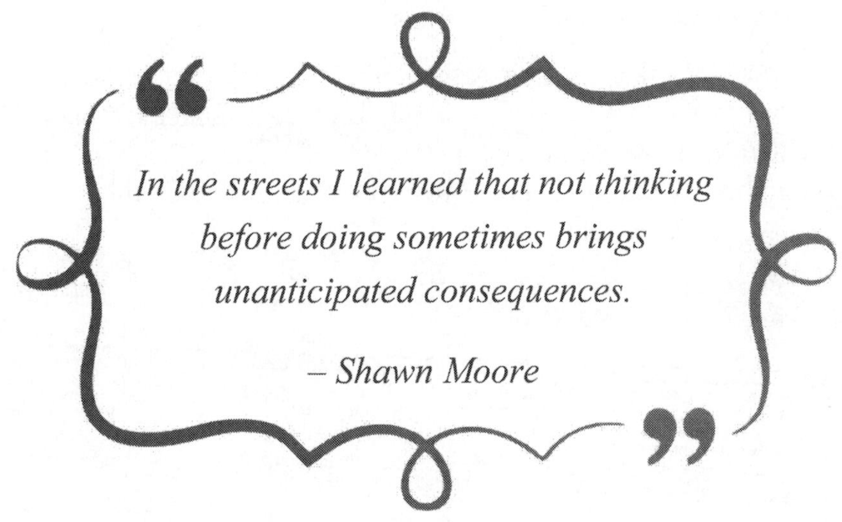
In the streets I learned that not thinking before doing sometimes brings unanticipated consequences.
– Shawn Moore

CHAPTER ONE

DECISIONS

I want you to know about where I came from so that you can understand my story and what is so extraordinary about where I am today. We must start at the beginning of my life. I was born on November 7, 1970, and grew up in Saginaw, Michigan. I lived with both of my biological parents, along with my sister and brother. It was in Saginaw, Michigan, where my dad met my mother. My parents were married in 1971 and are still together today.

My mother was one of sixteen children, with one sibling dying at birth. She and her remaining fourteen siblings grew up in Alabama in a house with only one bathroom! Can you imagine all of those people, all of those kids, and only one bathroom in the entire house? Mom is the quietest, content, patient, grateful, giving, and loving woman I have ever met in my life. My mom is the best Domestic Engineer I know.

My father, while living in Louisiana, lost his mother (my grandmother), his two sisters, and a brother in a house fire. Imagine: in one day my dad's life was turned upside down at the tender age of six. After that tragedy, his father (my grandfather) relocated his family to Saginaw, Michigan, where he found work at a manufacturing plant. When my father came of age, he joined the U.S. Army. Afterward, he followed in my grandfather's footsteps and worked in one of the many car manufacturing plants in the Saginaw area. Dad is a calm, outgoing, caring, generous, and hardworking man.

Hopefully, after reading the characteristics of these two people who raised me, you can understand how my personality was formed and the way I think. I rarely ever saw my parents upset except when dealing with their disobedient children, usually my sister and I. (My little brother was typically the innocent one in the family.)

My parents still live in Saginaw today. My sister lives in the Detroit area, and my brother relocated to Alabama. I currently live in Kansas City, Missouri. According to the 2013 United States Census, the city's population was 467,007. Kansas City stays ranked as one of America's Most Dangerous Cities to live in and has earned the nickname of Killer City. That is interesting, because the place where I grew up has a high crime rate as well.

Let me tell you about Saginaw, Michigan. It is about 100 miles north of Detroit. There was a time when you could make a good living working in the automotive industry, which is what most people who lived in Saginaw did. As the years passed, the plants closed one by one, and unemployment skyrocketed. When unemployment increases, socioeconomic problems related to poverty increase, which leads to high crime rates, including but not limited to crimes against persons and property.

According to the United States Census of 1970, the year I was born, the population of Saginaw was 220,419. In 1990, twenty years later, the population dropped to 69,536 and in 2010, the population decreased to 50,303. Since 2010, Saginaw, like Kansas City, is consistently ranked in the list one of America's Most Dangerous Cities to live. Residents call it "Sag-nasty."

To put that in perspective, Saginaw is considered to be as dangerous a place to live in as some of the larger cities known for their gang activity. According to the area's crime statistics, a person has a one in fifty chance of becoming the victim of a crime in Saginaw.

These dreary and depressing statistics might lead some to believe that if you live in Saginaw, you will not amount to much. There is a high probability that a Saginaw, Michigan, resident may not graduate from high school and may indeed visit the criminal justice system more than once, join a gang, experiment with and/or become addicted to drugs, and have a drinking problem.

Some people living in Saginaw or other comparable cities might believe there is no point in trying to better yourself. If you come from Saginaw or any other city like it, you may get the idea that you cannot be successful because there is too much stacked against you or the odds are not in your favor. Do you know of any successful people who were born in Saginaw, Michigan? You may be able to name a few; however, there are actually several famous and successful people born and raised in Saginaw. The Los Angeles Lakers head coach Darvin Ham, Stevie Wonder, and Serena Williams were born in Saginaw. Former Pittsburgh Steelers and Arizona Cardinals linebacker Lamarr Woodley, former pro football player Charles Rogers, former pro basketball players Jason Richardson and Mark Macon, and Golden State Warriors forward Draymond Green were born and raised in Saginaw. There are many high achievers, including professional athletes, actors, successful entrepreneurs, inventors, authors, and musicians, who once made their home in Saginaw.

The point I am trying to make is that where you were born or where you were raised does not determine the type of person you can become. Saginaw, Michigan, was not and is not an easy place to live. This city, like other metropolitan areas, has victims of unemployment, high crime rates, gangs, drugs, and alcoholism. These problems have touched everyone, directly or indirectly, in one way or the other. Escaping from these problems is what most people try to pursue every day. If you do not have musical talent like Stevie Wonder or athletic ability like Serena Williams, you have to find another way to succeed or to rise out of the problems that plague places like Saginaw.

Growing up, I was smart and an athlete who played basketball, soccer, and baseball. But rather than applying myself in school or using sports as a way out, I was too focused on trying to fit in and be cool. I was not unintelligent, but as you read this book, I will show you how intelligent people are capable of making some foolish decisions. So I turned to drugs, alcohol, and women as my means of escape.

By "escape," I don't necessarily mean the physical act of leaving the area. Oftentimes, I was trying to escape the feeling of not belonging and living up to the expectations of society. All I really wanted was to be loved and accepted, and I felt the streets provided that for me. In the streets, I wanted to be respected by my friends and my enemies. I wanted "street creds" and was almost willing to do just about whatever it took to get them. How far are you willing to go to get respect?

Like most kids in Saginaw, I attended public school. At age ten, I was being bullied at school. In an effort to protect me, my parents transferred me to a private school. Unfortunately, the move to a private school did not resolve anything. In the 1980s, here I was a black kid from the "hood"(according to some) attending a predominantly white private school! Although my parents meant well, they basically traded one set of problems for another. I felt like a zebra running from a lion that jumps into the water to escape the lion only to get eaten by a crocodile.

Therefore, my problems of being bullied followed me to the private school. At the private school, I rebelled against authority. At the age of fifteen, I was drinking alcohol. At the age of sixteen, I started to smoke weed, and experiment with sex, sneaking around, and carrying my dad's gun.

To say that I got into trouble is an understatement. I got myself expelled, kicked out of that special, unique, and predominantly white private school during my senior year of high school.

Let's be clear here. I could have easily said, "I got kicked out," giving the impression that it was not my fault, at least not all of it. I could have added that the administrators of that school didn't care about me and were out to get me because I am black. But that would not have been the truth. I have learned in life it doesn't do any good to have a victim mentality, because no one cares. The consequences are going to be the same whether I make up an excuse or not. At some point in your life, you have to stop playing the blame game and own up to your dumb decisions.

Are you blaming others for where you are in life, or do you take responsibility for your decisions? Are you a person who makes a lot of excuses, or are you learning from your mistakes?

I have to admit that I got myself kicked out because I was caught smoking weed, drinking, and messing with the girls when I knew it was against the rules. It didn't matter if the rules were fair or not. I knew what the rules were, and all I had to do was to obey them and graduate. Simple! But I made a choice, and I decided that what I wanted to do was more important than what they did not want me to do. I was rebellious, recalcitrant, childish, and certainly did not like people in positions of authority telling me what to do. Sound familiar?

Imagine how my life could have been if I had decided to listen to the authority in my life and follow the rules. I would have graduated on time and most likely would have avoided a lot of the problems I had. I am still suffering the consequences from some of the decisions I made. I am happy with how my life has turned out. But I have to be honest: I still have a lot of regrets.

Here I was, in my senior year, returning to the public school feeling abashed. To make matters worse, not all of my class credits from the private school transferred to the public school. This meant that in order for me to graduate, I had to attend another full school year. Now I'm back in a predominantly black school with the same kids from the same neighborhood. All of them knew I left to attend a private school. They knew I was the same age as they were and should be graduating with them, but I wasn't! Yes, I had to explain why I'm back and why I'm not graduating. This did nothing to help me fit in.

Still, I did not let that setback stop me from graduating from high school. According to statisticbrain.com, 90% of jobs require a high school diploma, and 75% of crimes are committed by a high school dropout. I didn't want to be a high school dropout because I knew I would be at a greater risk of getting in trouble. So I did what I had to do to make sure I walked across that stage to get my diploma. That was one of only a few good choices I made during that time.

While I was finishing up high school, I felt I had to prove that I did not think of myself better than everyone else just because I had attended a private school. Also, I wanted to prove to everyone that I was not "soft." So I started bragging about why I got kicked out. I then started hanging out with the kids from the neighborhood every day, whereas in the past it was every once in a while. Before transferring to the private school, I had attended Keoltzow Elementary School, where I got to know all the kids from my neighborhood. Now I was attending Buena Vista High School with the same kids that attended Keoltzow. We automatically had enemies at school just because of the area in which we lived. I thought this was unfair since I had no choice in the matter of where I lived, but I still had to deal with the consequences of it daily.

Have you ever made a choice, and at the time you thought it was your only option, only later to find out you had other options? In my mind, I had to connect with the guys in my neighborhood—which was unfortunate for me, because a lot of them were involved in the street life. I knew people who stayed clear from that lifestyle, who weren't doing drugs or in the streets. We called them squares, jocks, or outcasts. The fear of not being accepted was harder to overcome than the fear of living life in the streets.

Now that I am older, I realize that life is hard no matter which road you choose. It brought comfort to me to hang around my friends in my neighborhood with that common factor that held us together. We all had the same enemies based on the side of town we lived on. I knew they had my back, and I quickly learned I needed to have theirs as well. At age seventeen, nothing felt worse than being an outcast, so I began doing what my friends were doing just to fit in.

During that time in my life and for many years to come, my biggest fear was not going to jail or even dying. I feared being alone, being put down, spoken of in a negative way, and not being considered one of the guys. I feared having no friends and not being thought of as "cool." Those fears formed the foundation of the many bad decisions I would soon make. What about you? Are you afraid to be rejected by people? Do you ever let peer pressure force you to become someone other than yourself?

I believe that there is a basic desire within every human being to be accepted and to be included in a group of friends. No one likes to be on the outside looking in, and so we search for a way to be accepted into the group where we think the fun is. The only problem with that mindset is that what may be fun for today can—and usually does—result in heartache, pain, and regrets tomorrow. I was trying so hard to fit in and to make a name for myself that it almost cost me my freedom—not to mention my life.

In Chapter 2, I will show you how a few *dumb* decisions almost cost me my life and how, if I would have gone home to get my guns, I may have been in jeopardy of losing my freedom.

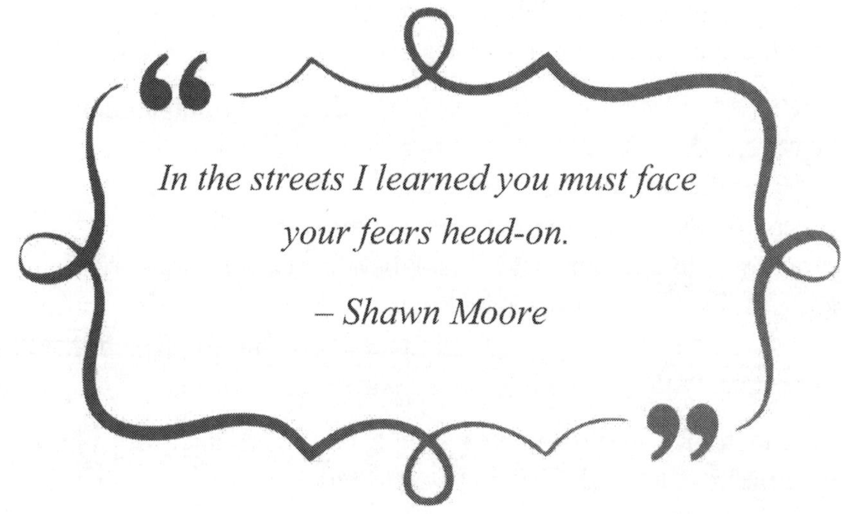
In the streets I learned you must face your fears head-on.
– Shawn Moore

CHAPTER TWO

DUMB

THIS DAY WAS NOTHING SPECIAL. It was approximately 1990, and I was twenty years old. I was at work, and my phone rang. I wasn't supposed to answer my phone on the job, but I did. And boy, I wish I hadn't. Tension and apprehension ran through my veins as I heard a familiar voice on the other end of the phone yelling and screaming at me.

My mind quickly raced back to about a month prior when my friend Cat, who reminds me of Morris Chestnut (he was a smooth fellow), called me to hang out with some friends. Cat was already with them. It was dumb for me not to listen to my conscience when I found out that Snake and Gorilla would not be with us, even though their girlfriends had come to hang out with us. I did not feel right hanging out with someone else's girlfriend without her boyfriend being around.

Snake was one of my good friends from the neighborhood. We were like Caine and O-Dogg in *Menace to Society*: we were tight and always together. Gorilla was cool, but I had only known him for a year or two. I shouldn't have gone, but I did.

Both of the girls were fine, really good-looking. So I succumbed to temptation. I wish I knew back then the verse in Proverbs 1:10 that says, "My son, if sinners entice you, do not consent." We hung out and had a good time. I was enjoying myself. I was spending time with Gorilla's girlfriend. The night ended with us messing around. I didn't think much of it. It was a one-time thing. Even though I wasn't in church then, I usually lived by the Golden Rule, found in Matthew 7:12, which says, "Whatever you want men to do to you, do also to them." Imagine how the world would be if everyone treated everybody else how they want to be treated.

A month later, here I am on the phone with Gorilla yelling and screaming at me, "How could you mess with my girl? I thought we were cool." I was shocked that he found out, and immediately, fear kicked in. Ice ran through my system. I already had enough enemies, and I was not trying to add any more to that list. But it seemed too late for that not to happen.

In the early 90s, most people did not have large caliber handguns unless they had a lot of money. Gorilla had a 9mm, and all I had was a .38 and a .380. I was at work, and my guns were at home.

My job was in Bridgeport, Michigan, one minute from the state police headquarters. They had a tendency of pulling people over just to check you out. So I rarely took my guns to work because of the possibility of getting pulled over and my car being searched.

Gorilla was staying with my friend Tiger at the time. During this phone conversation, Gorilla asked me to meet him at Tiger's house after I got off work. He wanted to talk to me about what had happened between me and his girl. I knew I was not in a good situation either way. My conscience told me to think through my choices. I could have called some of my friends to go with me, but then it would have appeared I was afraid to face him alone, and I didn't want anyone thinking I was afraid.

I could have decided to go home to get my guns first, but I wanted him to know that I came directly from work. Wanted to let him know I wasn't stalling. I was as real as they came, ready to face whatever happened. If I wanted to earn respect in the streets, this was a part of the process, or so I told myself. That process started with me believing I was hard before anyone else would know I was.

Deep down, I knew I was in the wrong. You should never mess with a man's girl. I wouldn't want anyone to disrespect me like that. My actions were disrespectful and came with unanticipated consequences, so I understood why Gorilla was so angry. Have you ever done anything that you later regretted? This is one of those decisions that I regretted later.

My conscience was bothering me after the phone call ended. Choices ran through my head, and I could not concentrate on work. I was faced with a tough decision. Do I go over there and face the consequences from my horrible decision, or do I avoid him and let him, and everyone else, think I was afraid? There was no way I could take the risk of him telling people I was scared to come talk to him.

This is what was running through my mind: If I did not go, he would think I was a punk. If I did go, he might kill me, or I might have to kill him. Either way, it was a lose/lose situation. I had about three hours before leaving work to decide what to do. I decided to go straight from work to Tiger's house without my guns.

But I wanted my guns with me! Wait. Gorilla did not know whether I had my guns or not. Everybody knew I kept a gun on me. So he should assume I had one now. I did not know what was going to happen. While driving over to Tiger's house, I thought this could quite possibly be my last day on this earth.

I was so afraid when I arrived. My heart was pounding out of my chest. I felt as though I was having a heart attack. My ears were ringing. Gorilla was waiting outside for me. He had this enraged look on his face. When I got out of the car, his expression changed to a look of surprise. It was as though he couldn't believe I would show up. We talked cordially. I then noticed it became difficult for him to talk to me. He became so angry that he began to tremble while he spoke. His eyes became darker, and he could not stand still. Shortly afterwards, one of his friends pulled up. I said to myself, this isn't good. Now it was the three of us, and Gorilla wanted us to go inside the house.

I didn't want to go inside, because his demeanor and the tone of his voice had changed. He looked like a different person. He started getting louder. Was Gorilla trying to impress his friend? He had a dangerous, killer look in his eyes. His pupils dilated, and he started to sweat rage from his pores. Again, I knew I was in the wrong. I wondered what would happen next. The only certainty for me was that I was not going to show any signs of weakness. So as my pulse pounded out of control, I went into the house with a cool (outer) demeanor.

Gorilla had already told his friend what happened between me and his girlfriend. He expressed again how I was wrong and that I was lucky that he was not going to do anything to me. I was so relieved to hear those words. He showed me his gun and said if he wanted to kill me, he could. When he was finished putting me in my place, he told me to leave. I couldn't leave that house fast enough.

When I got in my car, I couldn't believe that I was still alive. The tension inside me had built to a point where all I could do was laugh, and it was uncontrollable. Cold sweat dried on my skin, and I felt as though I'd just finished riding the Blue Streak at Cedar Point (a big amusement park in Sandusky, Ohio—I would have said "riding the Magnum," but that would have been a lie, because I was afraid then and I'm still afraid now to ride that roller coaster). I had survived and, for that day at least, had conquered my fear of dying or being killed by a man. I had faced my fear of being shot.

To some, going into the house was the bravest decision I could have made. To others, that was the dumbest. Remember, I had chosen the path of street life, which comes with good and bad consequences for the decisions we make. So whether it be jail or death, I was willing to suffer the consequences of what I had done. In my mind, it was all good. Now I see it was just dumb thinking. However, in this game, for me, there was no faking it.

The fear of not being accepted by my peers led me to face my fear of dying and deal with it once and for all.

What is fear keeping you from doing? Are you afraid to try and change because of fear of failing? Are you running from the results of bad choices, or are you blaming others rather than owning up to them yourself? Are you afraid to make different choices because of what someone else might think or say?

Not all fear is bad. Most times, fear is a good thing to have. It makes us think and evaluate our circumstances before doing something we shouldn't. Fear of killing someone, being killed, and going to prison for the rest of our lives are all good fears. Proverbs 1:7 says, "The fear of the Lord is the beginning of knowledge, but fools despise wisdom and instruction."

But here's the thing. It makes no sense to fear man or anything else in the world and not to fear the One who created all things. We as humans care way too much about what people think about us. Proverbs 29:25 says, "The fear of man brings a snare [a dangerous trap]: but whoever trusts in the Lord shall be safe." Hebrews 10:31 says, "It is a fearful thing to fall into the hands of the living God." Many never think about the day that they will have to stand before God and give an account of their deeds. But that day is coming.

This means we don't have time to be daydreaming and just living life any kind of way and not fearing the day we will die and have to see God. The time to make better choices and realize we can do better in life is now. Remember, some fears are good, but a fear of change is not one of them. A fear of change keeps us from becoming what we want to be, should be, could be, and are created to be.

What are you fearful of today? If you say, "Nothing," that is not a good answer. Keep in mind that not all fear is bad. I wish now I would have feared disappointing the people who really loved me more than I did. I hurt my mom and dad more than I care to think about. At the time, I didn't listen to or care about the people who really loved me and wanted me to do something with my life. I was fearful, but not of the right things.

What about you? I know someone may be saying, "I didn't have a mom and dad, so there's no one there for me to show respect." But if you look hard enough, you had someone in your life who loves you and cares for you and has given you good advice. I challenge you—don't be like me. I allowed fear to cause me to make some very dumb decisions.

My goal was to not have anyone think I was weak—no one at all. From that moment on, any decisions I made could have cost me my life or my freedom. That became the norm in my life if I was going to become the person I was trying to be. Hard.

I don't believe it was a coincidence that I survived not being killed that day. As you continue to read my story in chapter 3, I will show you how *dangerous* my life was becoming and why I fell in love with carrying guns.

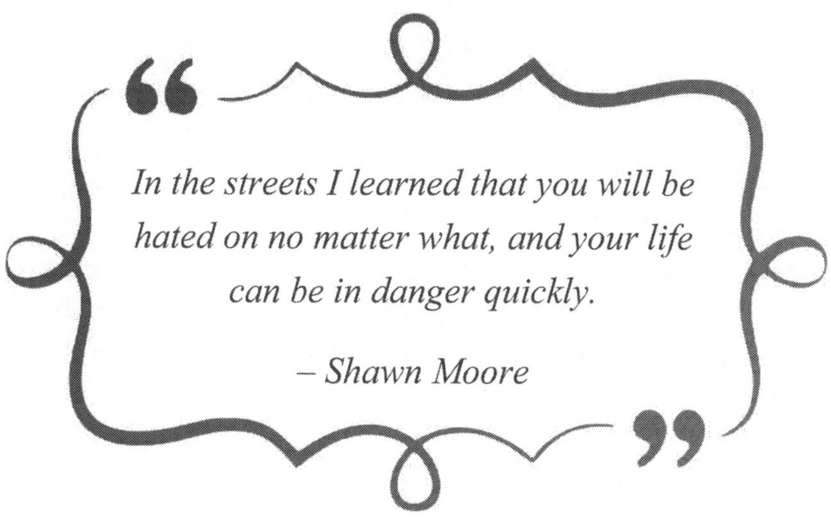
In the streets I learned that you will be hated on no matter what, and your life can be in danger quickly.
– Shawn Moore

CHAPTER THREE

DANGEROUS

DEATH IS NOT SOMETHING YOU WANT TO WAKE UP thinking about. Even though we all know we must die one day, it is hard to get our brain to wrap around that concept.

Around 1991, when I was twenty-one, I definitely was not thinking about dying. I was trying to get high. So I went to my friend Anaconda's house. It was okay to smoke weed there. My friend Snake went with me.

Anaconda had company. A girl from the neighborhood was there. Anaconda was not dating her. She was a cool friend with all of us. Anaconda noticed her talking to me a lot, and out of jealousy, he asked me to leave. I got mad because Snake, who came with me, was not asked to leave—just me!

I do not remember what I said to him, but whatever I said, he didn't like it. I wish I had known the verse in Ecclesiastes 3:7 where the author says there is "a time to rend [tear apart] and a time to sew; a time to keep silence, and a time to speak" (KJV). My mouth got me in so much trouble back in the day. What about you? Have you ever wished you weren't so quick to speak? Have you ever used your words to hurt someone and wished you had just been quiet? I wish I hadn't said anything to my friend Anaconda that day, but I did.

So now Anaconda challenged me to go outside and fight. He asked me to put my gun down and fight him. I needed him and others to know: don't get it twisted, I can use these hands if need be. Because he was a friend, I put my gun down. Like I said before, everybody knew I would have a gun on me, and I did.

The only reason I started carrying guns is because people had stopped fighting and started shooting. It used to be where two guys would get into a fight, and you might get hurt, but you would live to fight another day. But times were changing. People were dying. And I wasn't trying to be one of those who got killed. When the wintertime comes in Michigan, you better put your coat on. I saw that the streets were changing; therefore, I adapted to my environment and added a gun to my wardrobe.

Anaconda did not know that my parents had signed me up for karate lessons while I was attending the private school. I had gotten pretty good with defending myself with my bare hands. There was this one kid at the private school who loved the military, and for some reason he always picked on me. We fought often. Over the years, I got lots of experience fighting with him and others.

So I gladly accepted Anaconda's invitation to put my gun down and fight him. I took my gun out of my pocket and placed it on top of the car. As I was squaring off to fight him, he quickly pulled my hat down over my eyes. For a split second, I couldn't see anything. I was ready to fight, and now I was tricked.

Seeing nothing but darkness, I was alarmed. Dread ran through me as though a panic attack was heading my way. Suddenly, I felt his hands near my waist. That second, I knew where he was positioned: directly in front of me. I braced myself, ready to get hit in the face. But instead of wasting valuable seconds removing my cap, I swung. Hard.

I didn't know where my punch landed, but I knew I made contact, because I had a dull ache course through my knuckles. I lifted up my hat and saw he was on the ground. I hit him so hard that he took one look at me, got up, and ran inside the house. I thought it was over until I saw him coming out of the door with a long kitchen knife. I reached for my gun. It was gone. So I did what any real man would do. I ran. I ran hard and as fast as I could, not looking back at all.

I ran around the corner to Snake's house and banged on the door. His mom let me in, and I was glad she did. I then phoned Snake, who was still at Anaconda's house, to see if he had my gun. He did, so I asked him to bring it over to his house.

A few minutes later, there was a knock at the door. I opened it, and Anaconda was standing there. I quickly slammed the door in his face, agitated that it wasn't Snake, and waited for him to bring my gun. Truthfully, I was apprehensive, because Snake was both of our friends. I didn't know if Snake was going to give Anaconda my gun or bring my gun to me. In the streets you have to be on guard for anything. I don't know what Anaconda did when I slammed the door in his face, and truthfully, I didn't care. All I wanted was my gun.

When Snake arrived, I asked him why he took my gun. He said he didn't want me to shoot Anaconda. He asked me what I would have done if I had my gun. I told him, "You already know." But I do remember telling him that I didn't really want to shoot Anaconda. But if he would have tried to stab me with that knife, what was I to do? I was petrified of being stabbed with a knife.

Have you ever been in a situation where what could have happened didn't happen? This was one of those times for me. I now realize God was watching over me. Can you see times in your life where God was watching over you, and maybe you didn't realize it was God? Take a minute to recognize that and be thankful.

After evaluating the entire incident, I realized what Anaconda's hands were doing near my waist. He may have been reaching for the bottom of my coat to pull it up over my head while I was trying to remove my hat from my eyes. This strategy would have given him the advantage over me, and I would have been blind and bound. Smart.

You see, Anaconda was from the old school and spent time in prison. He weighed about 165; picture J. J. on *Good Times* but with about 20 more pounds, compared to my 275 pounds. He knew he could not have fought me equally. He had to have an advantage, an upper hand.

Looking back, I am grateful to Snake for taking my gun away, because this story could have had an entirely different ending. However, after that day, I never put my gun down to fight anyone ever again. I stayed strapped.

Facing death that day taught me not to trust anyone. Anaconda was one of my friends from the neighborhood, but because of a female, suddenly my life was in danger, again. I don't believe it was a stroke of luck that Snake took my gun that day. I do think it's odd that Anaconda didn't catch me. Even though I was running fast, I don't think I was running that fast. I don't know how far he chased me with that knife—like I said, I didn't look back at all until I got to the door of Snake's home.

In chapter 4 I will show you how *crazy* my way of thinking had become and how someone driving down a street could have completely changed the course of my life.

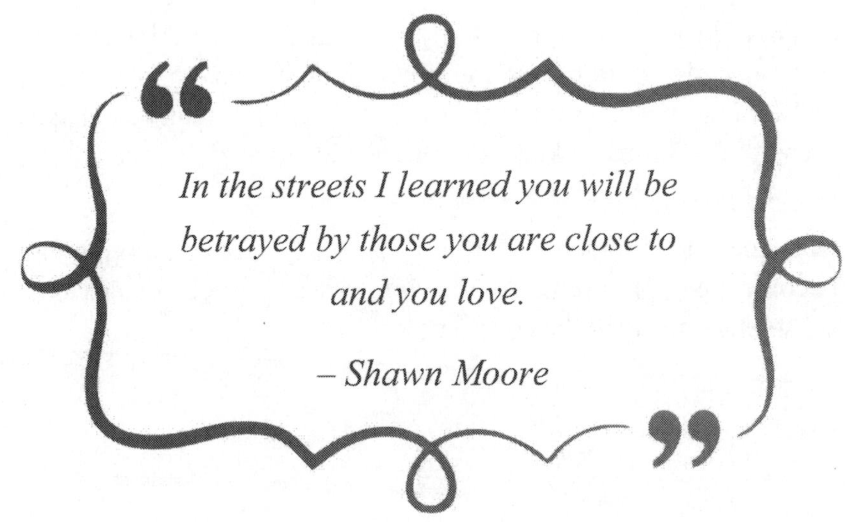
In the streets I learned you will be betrayed by those you are close to and you love.
– Shawn Moore

CHAPTER FOUR

CRAZY

THE TIME CAME FOR ME TO DO WHAT I really wanted and needed to do to get the respect I wanted in the streets. There were a few times in my life that I really thought I might kill someone. This was one of those times.

I was going to see my girlfriend of three years. It was around 1992, and I was about twenty-two years old at the time. While I was pulling up her driveway, I saw a car leaving. I asked her who was leaving, and she said that they were at the wrong house. She said they thought a party was going on. It sounded suspicious, but I did not think much more about it that night.

A month later, I caught the same car in her driveway again. Before they could pull out, I pulled up behind them to block the car from leaving. I got out, walked over to the car, and asked who they were and why they were there. Even though I knew the answers before I heard them.

One guy said something smart. And I got angry. It was like heat building up inside me, wanting to be let free. I thought to myself, "You're getting smart, and you're at *my* girl's house?" I told him, "Please, don't get smart with me right now. My head is not in a good place!" I lifted up my shirt and showed him my gun, turned, and went back to my car.

Really, I was angrier with her than with them. I got into my car and left, a sick feeling in my gut. I understand it better today why the psalmist said in Psalm 120:2, "Deliver my soul, O Lord, from lying lips and from a deceitful tongue." I have always struggled with being around people who don't tell the truth. I have always tried to be a man of my word even when I was in the streets. One thing I learned in the streets is that a lot of people just be talking. But not me. I was really trying to live it.

This guy and his friend chased me down the street. I'm thinking I am about to shoot this dude as my muscles tightened. He pulled his car up beside mine, and I rolled down the window to see what he had to say. He told me his side of the story. He told me that my girlfriend told him she didn't have a man. I told him it's all good then, just a misunderstanding. I went home to clear my head.

Let me tell you this. Saginaw is a small town. If you ride around a lot like I did, you are bound to see people sooner or later. So I'm just riding around, and I see Ant, and he looks at me and smiles. I said to myself, "No he didn't." I gave him a pass that day. The next time I saw him, he did the same thing. This time I had my boys with me, and I hit a U-turn and followed him.

Snake was in the car with me. After noticing what I just did, he asked me what's up. I told him that's the dude I caught over my girl's house. My friends Cat and Python were in a car following behind us. When I caught up to him, he was on the corner of Genessee and Weber buying fireworks. By the time I got to him, he was back in his car with one of his boys.

I got out of my car and ran up to his car window. I asked him, "Ant, what's up with this smiling every time you see me"? He told me he could smile at anyone he wanted to. I told him that was true. I also told him not to blame me for what was going to happen if he continued to disrespect me. Every time I saw him, he had this smug look on his face as if to say, I been with your girl.

Before I knew it, he was reaching under his seat, and my instinct was he's reaching for a gun. I quickly ran back to my car to get my guns. But Ant pulled off. And Snake, Cat, Python and I did not chase him. For one reason, it was daylight. I know people are getting killed today in the daytime, but we just weren't doing it like that in the '90s. Another reason: too many witnesses saw the confrontation. The last reason was that I really wasn't trying to go to jail that day. It was the holiday weekend. I was trying to enjoy myself.

Later that night, my girlfriend said Ant did not have a gun but was reaching for a machete. I told her that she let me down and she had put my life in danger. I was all about making money and staying lowkey. I told her that she jeopardized all of that and my situation was about to get ugly.

I know you are wondering why I was still with my girlfriend when it seems as if she was cheating. I can sum it up in one word…crazy. I was crazy to think that the relationship would change one day. She had told me over and over she wasn't going to be like my momma and stay at home, which was exactly what I was looking for—a Domestic Engineer, a stay-at-home mom, which I believe should be one of the most respected positions in the world and should not be looked down upon. I wanted to start a family one day and settle down, and there were some things about this girl that kept me tangled in this relationship because deep down inside I wanted it to work out, even though I knew it wouldn't. Have you ever stayed in a relationship longer than you should have hoping that a person would change? If you are not married, don't waste your time. Learn from others' mistakes.

One evening, my girlfriend went to the store, and I was at her house chillin' and smoking some weed while I waited for her to return. Her phone rang. I answered, and it was Ant. He called me stupid for being over there. I told him to come over to see how stupid I was. I was already high, not thinking clearly, mind clouded. I lit another joint, left the house with the front door open. I walked across the street smoking a joint with my guns in my hand. I left my car in her driveway.

There were some bushes across the street, so I laid in them to wait for my target. I called my friend, who lived eight houses down, and told him what I planned to do. I told him that after I finished this business, I would run to his house to hide out. Someone said best friends are people you don't need to talk to every single day. You don't need to talk to each other for weeks, but when you do, it's as if you'd never stopped talking. This was one of those friends.

I was so high that I did not realize that the killing I was planning would be easily solved by the cops. I was not firing on all cylinders. My car was in the driveway, and I had left the front door open.

That moment, I was so angry that the black hole of emotions consumed me, and I didn't care about anything, not about taking a person's life or about how I might get caught. I was in the dark, lying in wait in the bushes, smoking a joint, ready for him to come so I could end his life.

Every car's headlights I saw coming my way spiked my erratic heartbeat. Then I saw him, and my heart was pounding so hard it felt as though heavy hail was beating on my chest. I watched as he drove. And what did he do? He never turned down the street where my girlfriend lived. He did not turn and drive down the street where I was waiting to kill him dead. He drove right past the turn.

As I am writing this story, I am so glad Ant didn't turn down the street where I was waiting for him. If he had, I know I would have killed him or at least unloaded my guns trying. My goal at that time was to kill him. Hear what I am saying: I was high, and I thought I saw my man's car. Still to this day I don't really know for sure if it was him or not, but whoever was driving that car was probably going to get shot that night if things had gone a different way. That is why I am so against people shooting up cars and houses in the dark, which only leads to innocent people being killed.

Crazy thinking leads to crazy actions with little regards for the consequences of our decisions. It was so ironic that I saw Ant only one more time in my whole life. Don't know what happened to him. Did he move, was he dead, in prison? I look back now, and I am so grateful that I did not get the opportunity to do what I had planned to do that night. I don't believe it's a coincidence that I only saw him one more time in my life and that that car did not come down the street.

I was astonished at the person I had become. I saw that I was beginning to have very little respect for human life. Deep down inside I knew this feeling, this thought, was not a good thing. But I was in the game, there was no turning back. That fear of someone killing me only gave me a stronger desire to shoot first and ask questions later. That night was one of those nights. I was ready to do whatever was necessary to get respect.

Do you think the decisions I was making at this point were wise or foolish? What do you think about the decisions you or someone you know are currently making? Are they wise or foolish? Where are your choices in life taking you this very moment?

Can you see how crazy my life was turning out? In chapter 5, I will show you how I almost died from *illogical* thinking and impersonating a collection agent.

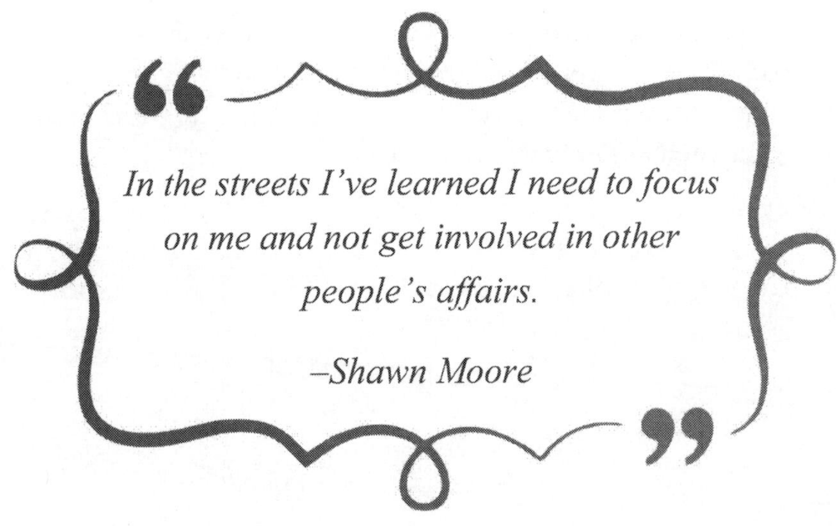
In the streets I've learned I need to focus on me and not get involved in other people's affairs.
–Shawn Moore

CHAPTER FIVE

ILLOGICAL

ONE EVENING I WAS HANGING OUT WITH MY friends Cat and Cobra. Cobra was Cat's cousin, and he was the man. Cobra was the one who introduced me to selling crack cocaine. Cobra thought he was Nino Brown, the godfather and big drug kingpin. He had big dreams. He thought his cousin Cat, a good friend of mine from the neighborhood, and I were going to help him reach his dreams. It's probably 1993, and I was about twenty-three years old at the time.

I loved hanging around Cobra because he had a business mindset and he loved having nice things. Nice cars, sounds, clothes, shoes, and jewelry: my kind of man. One thing about me, even though I needed attention and had a strong need to be accepted by my friends, I had my limits. They say money doesn't bring you happiness, but I say neither does being broke. That was my philosophy in the streets.

I have now learned that what the author in Proverbs said in chapter 22, the first verse, is so true, "A good name is to be chosen rather than great riches, loving favor rather than silver and gold."

What do people think about when they say your name? We need to be meticulous with the decisions we make, knowing our name will be affected by our behavior. But I didn't know that then. I had probably heard it, but I sure didn't know it.

For instance, I had some friends who just loved getting high. They would spend every dime they had to get high. Sometimes they would steal from family and friends. But I loved money and women too much for all that. I loved looking good, having nice clothes, shoes, jewelry, cars, and definitely money. And then I had to be around some females eventually. I couldn't stand just sitting in a room with men all day getting high.

In my mind, I was never going to be broke. I would do whatever it takes. This is why even though I was a hustler, I always worked a job, most of the time two. The jobs I took gave me the freedom to live the lifestyle I wanted. Most of the time I was even selling drugs on my job too. Despite many bad decisions, I am proud of the fact that I started working at the age of sixteen and have never stopped working. I have always had a strong work ethic. My first job was in the fields with my Hispanic friends, and we had to start early in the morning.

Back then, even when I was out all night, I rarely ever called in to work. I loved the fact that people could depend on me. This is why Cat and Cobra recruited me to help them achieve their agenda. Even when I was in the streets, I lived a life of integrity, except when it came to women.

Cobra had a circle of people he would give dope to on credit all through the month. At the first of every month, we would go to collect from them the money owed plus the interest. A $20 credit would end up being $35 or more. So you can imagine how much money we were collecting on the first of every month. These people were getting high every day. Business was good, including the transactions we took care of personally on a day-to-day basis all through the month.

Well, one day that I remember very clearly, Cobra told me and Cat about this man who would not pay his money. As it turns out, the man was married to Cobra's sister. But in this business, there are no free favors. So we went over to his sister's house to rough up her husband a bit.

Now, Cat is a strong dude. He had a 50-Cent type of body. When he hit you, it hurt. I weighed 275 and thought I was "all that" because of my size. So when her husband let us into the house, we grabbed him, threw him up against the kitchen cupboards, slapped him around a bit, and told him we weren't playing. We told him he better give Cobra his money or else. Eventually, he paid Cobra his money.

Months later, Cat, Cobra, and I were hanging out at Cobra's sister's house. I was rolling up a joint when Cobra's pager went off. He and Cat left to go around the corner to do a quick run. I stayed behind to roll joints. Hanging out with Cobra was risky because we always had a lot of dope on us. But Cobra was fearless. He played his music so loud and didn't even care about the police, which I thought was crazy, because we were always riding dirty. Back then the police would use the excuse of your music being too loud to pull you over all the time. So this is why I stayed behind to roll up joints.

While I was sitting there, I saw something out of the corner of my eye. It was Cobra's brother-in-law. At the time, my heart dropped in my chest. You'd think I would have known better. I knew I was slipping, and I was mad at myself because I always have my gun on me, and I knew better than to be in the wrong place at the wrong time. My heart was beating like when something runs out in front of your car unexpectedly and you have to slam on the brakes before you can even start thinking.

This man was a Vietnam vet, and he had this old gun in his hand. Here I am in his house, and he is about to get away with killing me. I had no way to defend myself.

He looked at me and said, "Where are your boys now"? Remember: they are all related, except me. I am an outsider in his eyes. I thought about trying to apologize just to get out of the house, but something told me not to say anything, and as a matter of fact, not even to look at him.

So I kept my head down and kept rolling joints as if he wasn't there. It worked! When I looked up, he was gone.

I knew he was still in the house somewhere, so I did not leave my seat until Cobra and Cat came back. I told them what happened, and they laughed. They laughed hard. I did not think it was funny at all; especially since I didn't get any pay for beating him up. Here I faced death once more. I think it was illogical for me to believe it was okay after we had just roughed up her husband for me to go back over there. This shows how wrong our thinking can be when we make excuses for ourselves or act like something doesn't matter.

Are you quick to get into other people's business? Proverbs 26:17 says, "He who passes by and meddles in a quarrel not his own is like one who takes a dog by the ears." In other words, it is foolish to grab a dog by the ears and think you won't get bit. The same is true concerning getting in other people's business. It's a big mistake to stick our nose in other people's business. I like to tell people, worry about yourself. That's a full-time job in itself. So don't get so involved in trying to fix other people's problems when you have problems of your own.

In life, we all make mistakes, but the problem with making mistakes in the streets is, some mistakes can cost you your life. Remember, the only reason I am sharing my story is to provide hope for the next generation. If I can change, anybody can change. I don't believe I was just fortunate that Cobra's brother-in-law did not kill me that day. I believe God was preserving me for his purpose and his glory.

In chapter 6, I will show you how taking *chances* can possibly change your life.

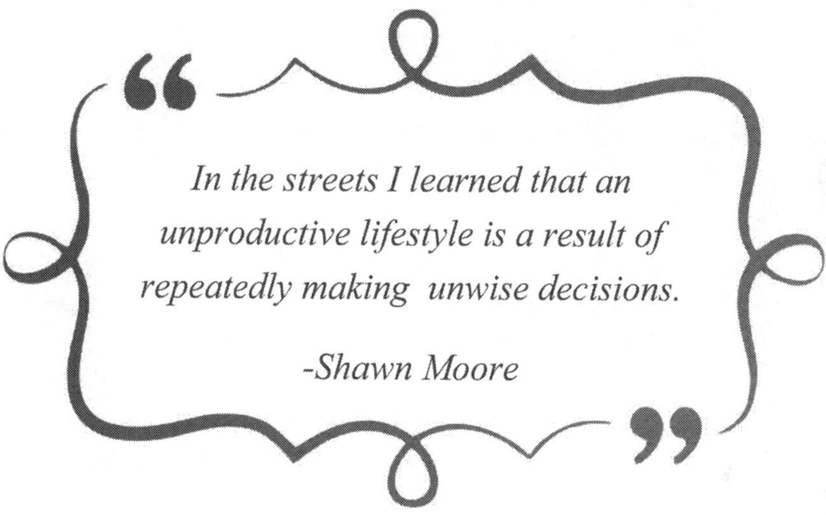

In the streets I learned that an unproductive lifestyle is a result of repeatedly making unwise decisions.

-Shawn Moore

CHAPTER SIX

CHANCES

In the neighborhood of 1998, when I was twenty-eight years old, I decided I needed to change. I wasn't happy with where my life was headed. There were very few times that I was sober, but in those times, I used to daydream about living a better life.

Do you have any dreams right now? I am telling you right now that dreams do come true if you learn to be disciplined and put in the work.

I had always wanted a house and a family. Yes, I could have had that at the time I was in the streets, but it would have made no sense to get married because all I would have done was cheat on my wife when things didn't go my way. Purchasing a home wouldn't have made sense either, because I was selling drugs, and it was just a matter of time before the police or feds would one day kick in my door and take everything I had worked hard for and relocate me to a new "place of residence" very quickly. I also juggled multiple girlfriends at the same time and didn't want any drama at my house.

So when I decided to change, I decided to change. I know this is going to sound crazy, but the first goal that I had was to stop selling and doing drugs. The second goal was to leave these women alone. I decided no more disrespecting women; I wasn't going to take advantage of women anymore. I wasn't going to use women to fulfill my selfish desires.

That decision was one of the hardest choices I ever made. Here I am, twenty-eight years old, saying I will not have sex again until I get married. I could be wrong, but I believe a lot of the problems we have in the world today are because of family dynamics. Very few love themselves enough to wait for someone who is disciplined and committed to the relationship. Too many settle like I did for years. According to a report released by the Urban Institute, the state of the African American family is worse today than it was in the 1960s.

In 1950, 17 percent of African American children lived in a home with their mother but not their father. By 2010, that had increased to 50 percent. In 1965, only 8 percent of childbirths in the black community occurred out of wedlock. In 2010, that figure was 41 percent, and today, the out-of-wedlock childbirth rate in the black community sits at an astounding 72 percent. The number of African American women married and living with their spouses was recorded as 53 percent in 1950. By 2010, it had dropped to 25 percent.

To change these stats, we need men who are disciplined and committed to marriage and their families. Discipline doesn't start when you get married. If you can't control yourself before you get married, you are going to have a hard time in your marriage. I always wanted to have a successful marriage, so I was committed to changing my ways so that when I found the right woman I would know how to treat her.

The whole point of me being so committed is because I wanted to be in the home. I wanted to be a husband and a father, even with the odds against me. I wanted to be a family man, despite what others were doing. I knew I wanted to follow in my dad's footsteps and be physically present in the home for my wife and kids.

We can see the effects of fatherlessness all throughout our nation. I know that kids often learn from observation. A young boy will learn how to become a man from being around a man. And the same is true for a little girl who has been influenced by a good mother. When I was growing up, there were many occasions I needed to just talk to my mom and, vice versa, in some situations, my dad. Life is hard, and on this journey, kids need much advice, guidance, and protection. I made so many mistakes as a young man and even more as I got older. So before I got married, I decided to become a better man. The decision to stop having sex was hard, but I knew it was the right decision.

So I went two years without actually having sexual intercourse, and then I messed up and went to hang out with one of my ex-girlfriends, thinking I was strong enough to say "no." I was wrong. After that day, I went ten years without having sex. During those ten years, I met my wife. This year, we will be celebrating fourteen years of marriage, which is so cool, because we spent seven years just being friends talking on the phone about life.

Our conversations were not about "I like you. Do you like me?" We were strictly friends up to 2009. At that point, I asked her if she was dating anyone, and she said no. I knew then that she was going to be my wife.

My wife was a 33-year-old virgin when I married her. She grew up in a God-fearing home with her four siblings. Her dad was a deacon, and her mom a godly woman, so when she told me she was a virgin, I was surprised, but not that surprised. I knew she was a person of good character.

It was at that time that I realized making wise decisions and taking a chance really did produce good results. Here I was, a man who made a lot of mistakes. But I had decided to make a hard decision at the age of twenty-eight, and fourteen years later, I was reaping the reward.

I am going to be honest, marriage is hard. My wife and I consistently read marriage books and set aside time to talk about marriage and what we are learning from our reading. Some of these conversations are intense but very beneficial. I am shocked at how many people get married and get comfortable and then say marriage doesn't work. Most of the time, it wasn't that marriage didn't work; it was that people weren't willing to put in the work.

If you are married, what are you doing to make sure your marriage doesn't grow stagnant?

My wife and I had been married for about a year when the phone rang and the voice on the other end said, "You are dead the next time I see you." I didn't know who it was. I didn't know if it was work-related, someone from the past, or just a prank call—but I wasn't going to take any chances. So I opened my safe, and grabbed my K, 9mm, and 12-gauge pistol grip pump. I already had my 40-cal out, because I slept with that by my bed.

I will never forget the tone in my wife's voice when she said, "It's 2 in the morning! What's going on?" She had this look of concern on her face. I bet she was thinking, "Who have I married, James Bond?" After I explained to her what the person said on the phone, I told her not to worry because I wasn't going to let anyone do anything to me or to her. If I could prevent it.

If you are wondering why I still had all these guns if I say I had changed, the answer is simple: I had changed, but the world that I left remained the same. Truthfully, it had gotten worse. We don't live in a world that respects people just because they have changed. I also don't believe that guns kill people. I believe people kill people. I believe in obeying the law. The law says I have the right to defend myself, within reason. So I'd rather take a chance at having a gun than not having one.

Oh, and by the way, another benefit of taking a chance: I had been able to hire a lawyer and get my record expunged, so all those guns were legit and legal. If I had a choice about whose family was going to have a funeral, someone is going to have to convince me why it should be my family. I was a man, not a thug or hard: just a man. As a man, I wasn't going to run from anything except maybe a dog, a snake, and maybe even a mouse. I will also run from a man if he has a gun and I don't have one. I realized what James said in chapter 4, verse 14, of his letter: "You do not know what will happen tomorrow. For what is your life? It is even a vapor that appears for a little time and then vanishes away." Life is already too short to be letting someone shorten it even more by killing me with a gun. I will never mind running to live another day.

But I am grateful that I am committed to *not* running from my marriage. Marriage is fueled by love, and love is a choice. We choose who we decide to show love to. I have made up my mind to love my wife unconditionally. That's what real men do. Yes, marriage is hard, but I am up for the challenge. I have appreciated being married because the institution itself has made me a better man.

I have enjoyed my new life with my wife. Shortly after getting married, we went to Jamaica on a cruise. Have you ever experienced going to sleep to the sound of the ocean crashing against the shore? I have, and I love it! I love looking out the window to a beautiful view of the water from a nice hotel. My wife and I were doing this before we had kids. Lolololololol. Now I have to find a babysitter to keep the closeness in our relationship.

I made a commitment to my wife fourteen years ago, and the plan is to stay faithful and focused on the task. I am no longer daydreaming about being a husband and a father. I am now living this dream. I have had the opportunity to be lead pastor at Bible Baptist Church, in Saginaw, Michigan, for six years, where God used us to impact many lives. Under God's guidance we were able to remodel the sanctuary and Sunday school rooms, and we went from having a window unit to having central air. Spiritually speaking, God did some great things in the place, with many souls surrendering to serve Christ.

In 2010, my wife and I relocated from Saginaw, Michigan, to Kansas City, Missouri, where we adopted three beautiful young kids. Both my sons were under the age of two when we adopted them, and my baby girl came to us straight from the hospital. Next to my relationship with God, my wife and kids are my main priority, and I love them so much. God has used our ministry and influence to help restore several broken relationships, including marriages that were once full of chaos only today to see them happily together because of the counsel of God.

If only people really understood Psalm 127:1, which says, "Unless the Lord builds the house, they labor in vain who build it." Marriages can only survive under the umbrella of both persons submitting to God's Word.

After you finish reading my story, I know you will realize life is not about *getting* a chance. It's about taking chances. I am encouraging you to take chances, because you never know how your life may turn out. And when I say "take chances," I don't mean doing something that puts yourself in danger or taking risks for no reason. But I do mean having the courage to make a change, having the courage to step out in faith. Since I made the decision to relocate to Kansas City, Missouri to serve in the role of assistant pastor, I was just recently voted in, after twelve years, as the lead pastor of Bannister Road Baptist Church. I desire to continue to be an example to show that the Word of God works if we believe.

So what is it that you are thinking about doing but you have been procrastinating? Don't fear failure. Do decide to embrace challenges and determine to take good risks. The life I am living today is not just for me. It is for anyone who dares to believe and is willing to act with courage.

Here I am living an entirely different life than the one I was living before. How did that happen? I was willing to take a chance that putting in the work would result in good things. None of this would have been possible if I had not decided to take a chance.

In chapter 7, I will show you how I almost put myself in the position to go to prison for the rest of my life because I was so determined to be *real*.

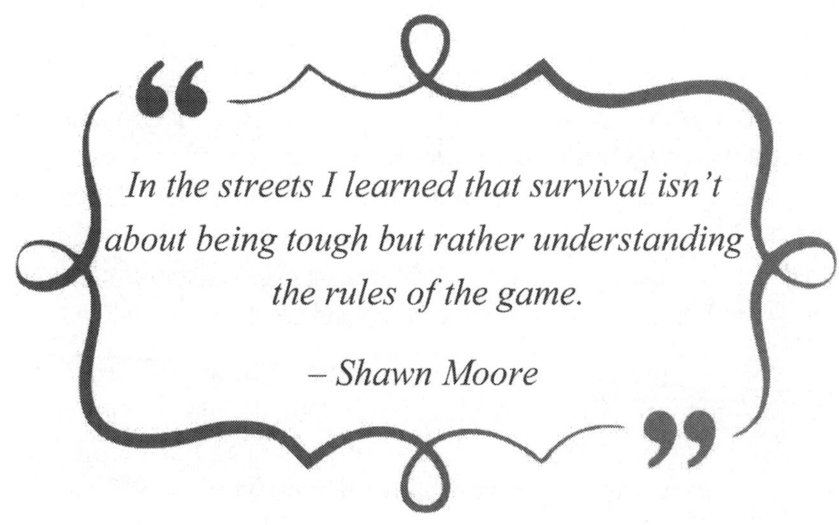

In the streets I learned that survival isn't about being tough but rather understanding the rules of the game.

– Shawn Moore

CHAPTER SEVEN

REAL

Hanging out past midnight was a goal I had when I was sixteen. The year is 1990, and I am twenty years old and still living at home with my parents. My parents were strict, so that goal wasn't reached, even at age twenty, unless I was with my older cousin, Teddy.

Teddy had two nicknames, one because of his size and the other because of his habits. Teddy was what we would call an "O.G.", original gangster. O.G. means someone who has put in work and has earned their respect in the streets.

Teddy loved the streets. He stayed in the streets. He always had a clean car with rims and sounds. He was a hustler with a capital "H," for real. Teddy knew fifty different ways to make money. He was never going to be broke for an extended amount of time. Many called him "D-Money" because he loved to pull out a lot of money and count it in front of everybody or take out a pile of bills and go through the entire roll of hundreds to get down to the fives and ones to pay for something in the store. I told him several times, you are going to get us robbed, man. He would laugh and say, "Not with you." He also had a gun on him most of the time as well.

So I was twenty years old, hanging out with D-Money. I loved hanging out with him. Spending time with him gave me some street credentials, "creds." He was well-known throughout the city. He wasn't afraid to go to jail like I was. He actually spent a lot of time in jail and did over seven years in prison.

While hanging with my cousin, I learned a lot about the streets. Teddy told me if I have a problem with someone, never handle my business when my enemy is with his boys. Always wait to catch him by himself, and ten out of ten times he would sing a different song. Once I tried that advice, and it worked. I was hooked with catching people by themselves. Totally different from the way they doing it in the streets today. He also taught me how to behave and act when I am around some real street cats. He told me to never be afraid of anyone—respect them, yes, afraid, never! You are as crazy as them. What can they do to you that you can't do to them? He also helped me to overcome some of my fears when hanging out in some crazy spots like 3rd and Potter, Projects, Lapeer Street, and of course the car wash on Genesee.

It was late one night, and we were on Genesee Street, called "the strip," where everybody hung out. While hanging out at the car wash, Teddy began shooting dice with some O.G.'s, and soon the arguing began. I remember him telling me to go to the car and get the gun. It felt so good for me to stand there and watch his back, and if anything went down, I knew he would handle the situation—or else I would have to shoot someone for the first time. Either way, we were going to do what we had to do together to survive that night.

Hanging with Teddy taught me to survive every night. Being around him made me feel real good, because the more people you know, the more respect and love you get on the streets. Through Teddy, I got to know a lot of older cats from the city.

One night, the phone rang. It was 1 in the morning. Teddy told me he just got jumped and for me to bring my gun. It was nothing for me to jump out of bed to go and make sure he was all right. For some reason, it could have been fear of going to jail—it certainly wasn't fear of killing someone—I went without taking my gun, because I knew if the guys who jumped my cousin were there, we were going to kill someone. And ultimately, I knew that that was wrong. Proverbs 10:27 says, "The fear of the Lord prolongs days." Even though I wasn't in church, I have always had respect for what

God said in the Bible. If I didn't respect the words "thou shalt not kill," there is no way I would be where and who I am today.

My cousin was angry, and he didn't play. I made a dumb but brave decision and went to meet him without my gun. When I look back at the night I probably didn't take my gun because I was awakened out of my sleep and not thinking straight.

When I got there, he told me that four men had jumped him and that he had lost his gold jewelry during the scuffle. We went back to the house where the fight took place. With flashlights, we looked around outside for his gold, not knowing if these men were in the house or gone.

Most people would have called the police and let them take care of it. In the streets, that is not how things are done. Situations like this we handle ourselves. It's called street justice.

There were times in my life that I was willing to do something to someone in spite of what I knew the Word of God said. But I wanted to be wise about it, hoping that I wouldn't get caught. However, the decisions I was making were very unwise.

The following days and nights, I took it upon myself to look for the dudes who jumped my cousin. Every time I rode past the house, I was searching for them. One day I drove my Cadillac past the house where my cousin had been jumped. I was listening to my beat, high as ever, and I saw this dude who didn't like my cousin because of a girl. He jumped off the porch and started running toward my car. Either that girl told him what kind of car I drove, or word got out that I was looking for the dudes who jumped Teddy.

I slowed down to see what this fool was going to do. To my surprise, he kept coming toward my car. He probably was going to try to do more to me, like he did my cousin. So I pulled off and went home to get my gun. I called my cousin and told him what happened. My cousin laughed and told me to shoot him. Normally, there were very few times I would leave the house without my gun. That night I got caught with my pants down. I was slipping.

I am nothing like my cousin. I was soft, trying to be hard. Truthfully, I was a little crazy as well, a walking contradiction. I wanted to be a good person, but it's hard to be a good person and live the street life at the same time. The street life will mold you into someone unrecognizable because the streets require you to be mean. Nobody smiles in the hood unless you are amongst friends.

My cousin was the real deal. Don't forget, the goal for me was to become hard. So I had to do whatever it took to get that respect from those streets. I got my gun, wiped off all my bullets, put my gloves on, rolled me a joint, and smoked it on my way back to find him.

There I am, about a block from the house. My heart is pounding so loud and hard that it drowns out the music playing in the car. I was listening to "Ambitionz Az a Ridah," by Tupac. Those in the street know what time it was. I knew that this is it. I'm about to shoot him in his face, and I am going to get out of the car and keep shooting.

I get to the street and slow down, approaching the house. Nobody is there. I said to myself, you have got to be kidding me. It's only been about 35 minutes. I was so amped up and mad because he wasn't there.

Looking back on my life then and on my life now, I'm grateful that nobody was on that porch when I drove back over there. I am grateful that I had to go home and get my gun instead of having it on me like usual. My life could have gone in a different direction if anyone had been outside that house that day.

Back then, I was putting myself in situations that could have cost me my freedom and possibly my life. Are you making any choices right now that are putting your life in jeopardy? I would advise you to think about your choices. Sometimes we don't get a second chance.

It wasn't an accident that I left my gun at home and that the guys who jumped my cousin weren't there that night or when I drove back by the house. In chapter 8, I will show you how I was as *reliable* as they come.

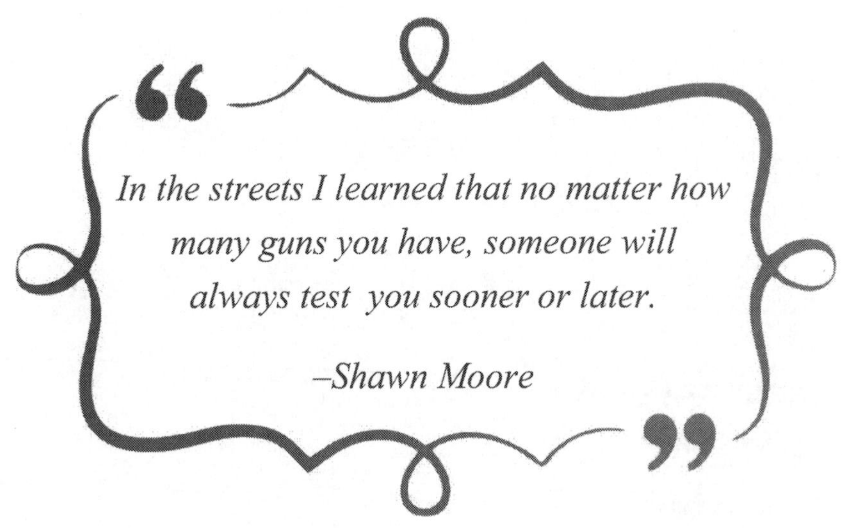

In the streets I learned that no matter how many guns you have, someone will always test you sooner or later.
–Shawn Moore

CHAPTER EIGHT

RELIABLE

Just another day in the hood. My friend Jaguar got locked up. He asked me to keep his guns for him while he was in jail. I already had three guns of my own, two .38s and a .32. He had a .380 and a brand new 9mm.

I felt invincible. I had five guns on me, thinking I was the man, not realizing I could have been doing twenty years for having five guns on me in Michigan.

I remember one day going over to my friend Tiger's house. It is in the neighborhood of 1994, and I am around twenty-four years old. Tiger asked to see my guns. I gave him the two .38s, and he said, in front of everybody, "What are you going to do now that I have your guns?" I remember how good it felt to go in my pockets and pull out the .380 and the nine. The whole house went crazy. They were like "This dude is crazy! How many guns do you have on you?" I said "five" with great pride.

What about you? What are you doing right now to impress people? Don't live your life trying to impress people. Spend more time trying to impress God.

My friend Jaguar ended up getting more time than he thought he would, so he sent one of his friends, Fly, over to my house for his guns.

Now, I don't know this dude at all; for all I know, he could be the police. So I told him I wasn't giving him any guns. I told him to tell Jaguar I would give him his guns personally when he gets home, and that is exactly what I did. At the time, I guess Jaguar didn't know if he could trust me or not. When Jaguar came home, I returned to him both of his guns. I wanted him to know I was reliable. I could have done like everyone else and lied or come up with some story about how I had to throw his gun, but that wasn't in my nature. Real cats don't steal from their boys.

I was mad that Jaguar sent Fly. I thought Jaguar should have known he could trust me, and he knew how I was rolling. I didn't like people coming to my house that I didn't know.

I guess Fly was supposed to be tough. He was trying to start up this gang, and he took offense to the fact that I would not give him the guns.

So I start hearing around town that Fly was going to do something to me for not giving him the guns. I said to myself, "He already knows what I have, so all he has to do is come and see me."

Some months passed by. I go to one of my friend's party, and guess who I see at the party? That's right—Fly and about eight of his homeboys. I wasn't too concerned because there were over fifty of us in the house, and we were all close. So I got high and drunk, just having a good time, and as I was sitting at the table, I noticed one of his little followers was giving me the finger. I was so drunk that at that instant I was actually afraid, because I could hardly stand up or see straight.

So I went and told my friend Snake what had happened and told him to be ready just in case something popped off. He said don't worry about that, it was too many of us for anyone to think of doing something to any of us.

But I always knew that if someone started shooting, there is only so much your friends can do for you in the moment. So I went into the bathroom and took out my gun, the 9mm, and put one in the chamber so that I could be ready to fire at any time. I remember saying in my heart, "I am going to kill one of these dudes tonight if they run up on me. I'm going to shoot everybody and anything that is moving. I'm going to just keep shooting period."

I had a seventeen-shot nine. I felt invincible. At the time I wasn't thinking about my family, the family of these guys, the police, jail, or the one hundred witnesses that were in the building. All I was thinking about was that my heart was beating like I was in a dark room by myself, and I saw something move.

Here I am in this situation where I can't leave because people will think that I am scared or that I was a punk. So I decided to stay, which put my life and freedom on the line. I actually stayed till the end of the night. It was 2 in the morning, and to my surprise, they never tried anything. But I stayed close to my boys that night, and I escaped another night—because I really believed I was going to kill someone if they ran up on me.

Looking back over my life, I am so grateful they did not test me that night. You better believe that version of Shawn Moore was going to pass the test. Some might imagine that the way things worked out was just fate. I don't think so; I was having too many close calls. Too many close calls that could have ended differently, but yet they ended well.

In chapter 9, I will show you how *ridiculous* I had started behaving.

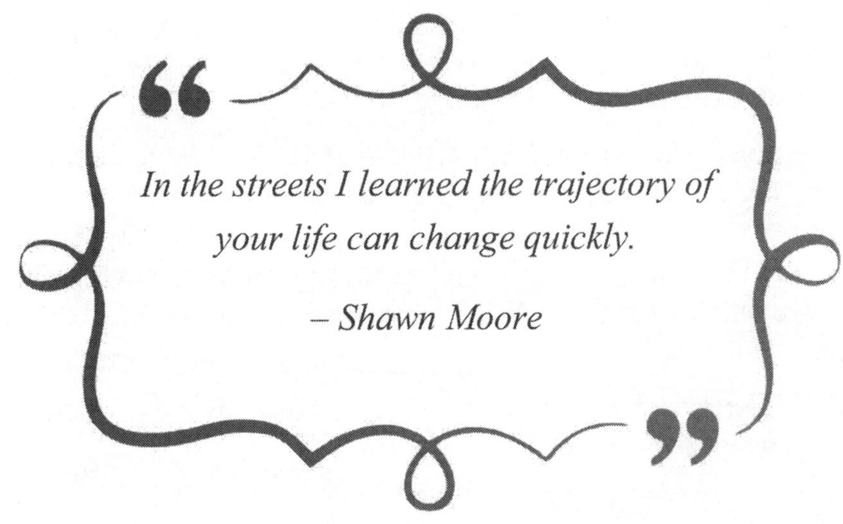
In the streets I learned the trajectory of your life can change quickly.
– Shawn Moore

CHAPTER NINE

RIDICULOUS

I bought my first gun at the age of seventeen. The year is around 1987. It was a nine-shot .22 that I bought from one of my cousin Teddy's friends. This was the gun I used in my first and only drive-by. I don't remember that entire incident, but I do remember somebody had done something disrespectful to one of my friends. So we got high and drove by the guy's house and got out of the car and took turns shooting at the house.

I remember being so afraid of getting caught and going to jail for shooting up a house with a .22, not knowing who was inside. I was so relieved to watch and hear on the news that no one got shot. I never told my friends how I really felt. At the time I was shooting, I just didn't care, because I had to let my friends know that I was down for whatever. How ridiculous it is to shoot into a house without knowing who's inside?

Proverbs 12:6–8 says, "The words of the wicked are, 'Lie in wait for blood,' but the mouth of the upright will deliver them. The wicked are overthrown and are no more, but the house of the righteous will stand. A man will be commended according to his wisdom, but he who is of a perverse heart will be despised."

I wish I would have used wisdom when that same .22 was with me the night I went up to a local school in my neighborhood. This rival gang just happened to be outside on the sidewalk. There were over a hundred of them just standing there looking at me, and three of my friends in a Pontiac 1000. They knew exactly who we were. We lived in a small town, and I was always hanging out. And with this new gun on me, I was itching to use it.

Once again, in the streets, the more work you put in, the more respect you get. So I knew I had to be willing to put in work, because I was craving respect. So we are sitting in the car looking at them, and they are looking at us. We were stuck in traffic because the parking lot was jam-packed. Suddenly, traffic started moving.

This was on a Friday night at a game at a local middle school. When we went back to school Monday, one of the guys who was related to one of the gang members told me we were lucky we pulled off when we did because they were going to bum-rush my car. I told him I'm glad they didn't bum-rush my car because I would have shot somebody. Period!

I have to say that life in the streets is not fair. The streets will force you to do things you might not want to do. Deep down inside, I didn't want to shoot anyone, but I couldn't allow myself to be scared to come outside or to go certain places. Who is going to respect you when you are afraid to go places because of the fear of being shot or jumped? I always felt like here I am a cool dude, but I got to watch my back just because of what side of town I live on. You tell me—how is that fair?

I don't believe I was just fortunate that they did not bum-rush my car and force me to shoot someone. In chapter 10, I will show you how *unintelligent* my decisions were becoming.

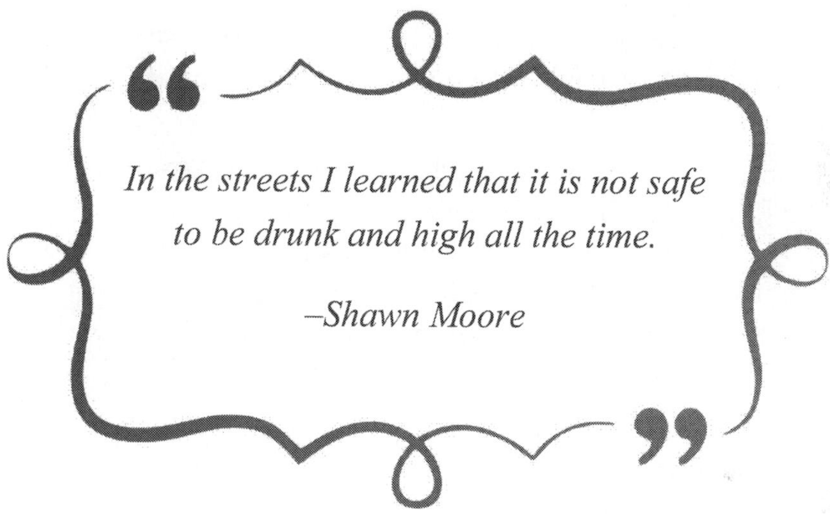
In the streets I learned that it is not safe to be drunk and high all the time.
–Shawn Moore

CHAPTER TEN

CLOSE

One of my friends, Cheetah, was just like me. The year is roughly 1993, and I am twenty-three years old. Cheetah always had a gun on him. Actually, he was a little worse, because he had been put in the situation to actually use his guns. Because of that, he had clout in the streets.

I remember a day Cheetah and I were talking, and he was so happy that he had four guns. We went to a party with three of our friends (Python, Lion, and Worm), and he was able to give all three of them a gun. They were all strapped with his guns: a .44, .357, .38, and a .22. The .44 had a 7.5-inch barrel, like Clint Eastwood used to carry in his *Dirty Harry* movies.

At the time, I only had a little .380 and a .38, and my friend Cheetah would let certain people in the hood borrow a gun from time to time. Especially those he knew wouldn't come back with no made-up story about why they had to throw the gun and they don't have it anymore.

He knew I wasn't like that. I was loyal, true, trustworthy, and not a liar. I had the privilege to keep the .44 on several occasions. This particular day, I was coming home from picking up my daughter (more on this below). At the time she was only about thirteen months old. As I was riding past a store on Genessee Street, one of the guys I went to school with (who was related to one of the gang members who didn't like me because of the neighborhood I grew up in) threw his hands in the air to me like saying "what's up!"

I didn't know what he wanted or his intentions, but I knew that in the store he was at, people were getting jumped and shot all the time. There was no way I was going to stop up there with my young baby in the car. So I put my finger out the window as to say I will be back in one minute … give me a minute. Then I floored it home got the .44 and dropped my baby off at my mom's.

By the way, the humor in this story is that I took care of this child for five years. When I lost my job and the mother demanded I take a blood test because she was trying to get child support from me after I fell behind, come to find out, the baby wasn't mine. My family was devastated. I know I am wrong in this, but all I could think about at the time was saving some money. My parents still have her pictures up in their home today. We loved that baby. But here I am leaving the baby with my mom to see what this guy wanted with me.

I went around the corner to pick up one of my boys to go with me. Python told me no, but Lion came with me. So Lion and I go back up to the store, and my man was gone. So I told Lion, let's ride by his house. So we did, and when we got there, he had at least thirty people in the yard with him. We rode past real slow, just letting him know that if he wanted some trouble, I wasn't hiding. Truthfully, I was foolish, because we only had six shots with that .44, and the odds were that out of thirty, at least six of them were strapped. I quickly took Lion home and thanked him for coming with me.

A few months had gone by, and Cheetah and I were hanging out. And guess what we had with us. You are right, the .44. We are drunk and high, having a good time. Cheetah says he is hungry, and so we decided to go to Bridgeport to get something to eat.

Bridgeport was the good side of town, so you know where this story is going. We make the decision to drop the .44 off at home and then go get something to eat. It was about 2 in the morning. As we were driving, the state police pulled us over and asked to search the truck.

As he was searching, he found some .44 bullets and asked where the .44 was. Cheetah told him it was his brother's gun. He probably had it at home. Fifteen minutes earlier, we had that gun in the truck with us. We both had enemies, and having a gun guaranteed some protection. I don't think it's a coincidence that we were that close to being caught with that gun.

When you live the life I have lived and have seen so many get locked up and murdered in the streets, I can't help but feel the pain of all those who are locked up or headed in that direction when I have had so many close calls myself. I had to make a change. Proverbs 10:1 says, "A wise son makes a glad father, but a foolish son is the grief of his mother." Today, my parents are so proud of me. What are you doing right now to make the people that love you the most proud?

In chapter 11, I will show you how me hanging out with my *friends* landed me in jail.

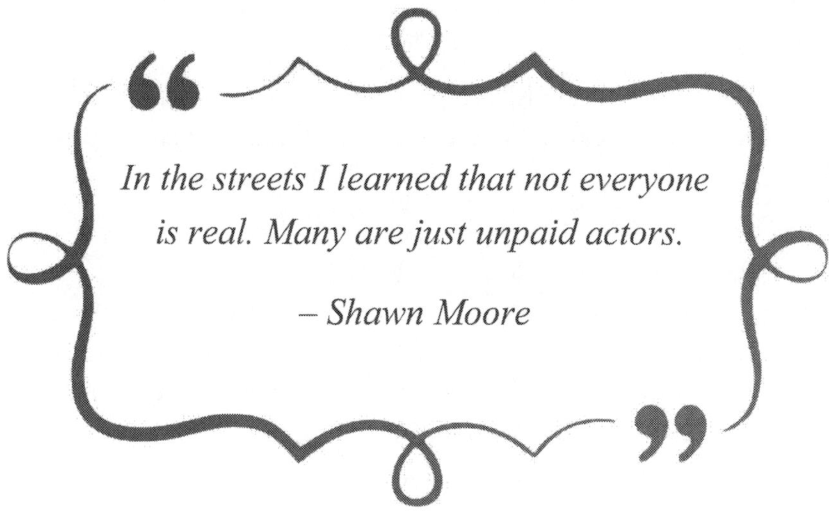
In the streets I learned that not everyone
is real. Many are just unpaid actors.
– Shawn Moore

CHAPTER ELEVEN

FRIENDS

Nothing felt better than knowing that someone we were close to was having a party. The year is around 1990, and I am twenty years old.

This was one of those nights, and I couldn't wait. I always felt safe at these parties because I knew that if anything happened, the odds were in our favor, so I could relax and enjoy my buzz.

This was a house party hosted by Cheetah's cousin, and everybody was there: Snake, Anaconda, Worm, Tiger, Crocodile, Cat, Python, Lion, and so many more. Everyone was having a good time. Sometime around 12:30 a.m., Tiger had done something to offend Donkey and Monkey, so they were going to fight him, not knowing that Tiger was with us.

All of a sudden, I heard the words "it's going down," and next thing I know, we were all fighting just Donkey and Monkey. There was no way they could beat all of us. So there really was no need for what happened next.

Python, who is the real deal, pulls out the .44 that Cheetah would let us carry from time to time and started pistol whipping Donkey. I will never forget the sound of that gun going up against the head of Donkey again and again and several times after that and all the blood that was flowing from his head. I remember hearing screams from many different voices and seeing people running everywhere.

You guessed it, the party was over, so I quickly ran to my car, and Worm came with me while everyone else went their separate ways. All we could hear were sirens. When I turned the corner, you could see nothing but lights, and I saw the police hit the U-turn. I knew they were going to pull us over. I wasn't too concerned, because in my mind, we weren't the ones who pistol whipped anyone, and I did not have the .44—but I did have my dad's .32.

When I made the decision to carry my dad's gun for protection, at first it seemed like a good idea, until I realized that decision was probably going to land me in jail. My dad kept his .32 in his dresser drawer, and for years I had been sneaking and carrying it for protection. My dad never knew I was stealing his gun. He actually thought it didn't work, so when they called him and told him, "Mr. Moore, we have your son," he told them, "You are mistaken." They asked him to go check his drawer. He did, and to his surprise he had to say the words, "Yes, you have my son, and my gun is missing."

When they pulled Worm and I over, the .32 was under Worm's seat because I threw it there when we first got in the car, but I told them it was my gun, which it was. I had never been arrested before and really wasn't trying to be. This was going to be my first time going to jail.

Like I said in the beginning of the book, I have had friends tell me they cried in the shower in prison out of fear of someone seeing them crying. I didn't cry, but I sure was disappointed in myself. A prison number does not have the same clout as a degree. In the real world, jail doesn't look good on your resume. People need to tell the truth about getting locked up. Most sane people can't wait to get out.

I definitely didn't like the interrogation part. I was adamant when it came to snitching. Yes, I knew what happened, but there was no way I was going to talk. I was willing to do whatever time necessary to not be known as a snitch. I grew up in the era where we were taught *snitches get stiches or end up in ditches*. All I could think about was getting out of jail quickly, but not at the expense of snitching.

It did not take me long to realize that jail was not for me. Life in jail isn't fair. You need to know someone to get a favor. Three people left and a new guy came in, but because he knew somebody who was already there, he got one of the beds that was available even though some others and I were next in line to get beds. I did not want to add another charge for fighting for a bed, so I just chilled and thought to myself, this mess is crazy.

In jail, I had to sleep on the floor due to over-crowdedness, and I traded my trays of food for chips, so I was hungry. Anyone who knows me knows that I am a picky eater, and I love to eat. The only comfort for me was that Worm and Tiger were in the cell with me, and a few more of my friends were locked up as well.

I remember Tiger's parents coming to get him, and then Worm's parents came. I called my parents crying and begging for them to not leave me there. After three days, my parents finally came and got me, and I thought I had learned my lesson. I did love the lifestyle, but I didn't like the consequences.. I hated the fact that I couldn't have my gun in jail, and sleeping on the floor wasn't cool. Not to mention the food.

Now, this is the part of the story that doesn't make sense. I didn't want to be locked up. I didn't like being locked up. But still, I didn't change my lifestyle. In fact, I actually started doing *more* wrong. I kept hanging around the same people and doing the same thing even after I got out of jail.

The decisions I was making could have landed me in jail for a long time. I started selling more drugs and carrying more guns after I was sentenced to probation for attempted Carrying a Concealed Weapon with the plea. I wish I could say them giving me a second chance helped me, but it didn't. I only got worse. Proverbs 11:14 says, "Where there is no counsel, the people fall; but in the multitude of counselors there is safety." I really wish I had a bunch of wise older men in my life to seek advice from, because I was stuck on foolishness and didn't want to listen to my dad.

Somehow, even though I didn't make right decisions, I only went to jail one more time in my life for about three hours for having some weed.

Someone said don't lose hope. You never know what tomorrow will bring. In Chapter 12, I will show you how having a little glimpse of *hope* paid off for me.

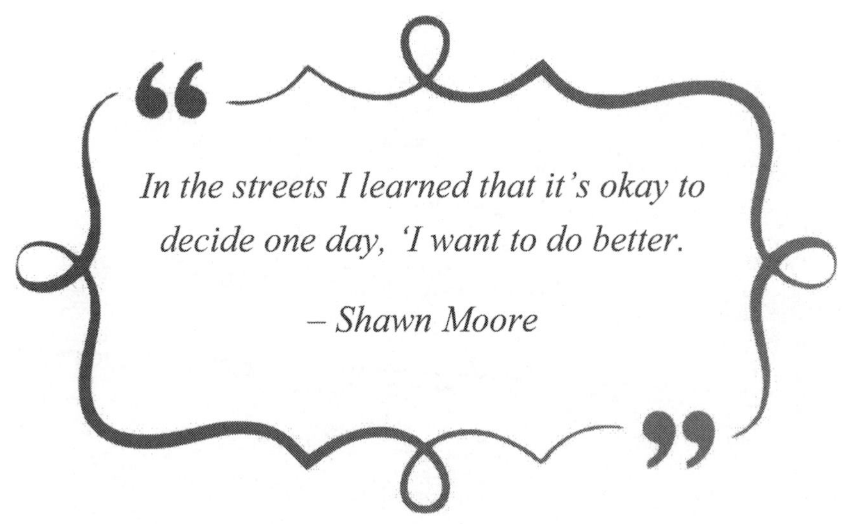
“
In the streets I learned that it’s okay to decide one day, ‘I want to do better.
– Shawn Moore
”

CHAPTER TWELVE

HOPE

The year is 1998, and deep down inside I knew I could do more with my life than what I was. I am twenty-eight years old, with no assets really, and my future seems hopeless. I am angry, depressed, confused, lost, and I have no life-changing goals. I said to myself, if I am ever going to change, the time is now.

So I decided to stop selling and using drugs. I decided to stop hanging around my friends from the street all the time like I used to. I wasn't going to be involved in illegal activities anymore.

This was a hard decision, because I loved having money and things. But the only thing I loved more than money was my freedom. I felt in my heart if I didn't change, I was going to end up locked up or dead. So I took a chance and decided to try to change. If we don't allow adversity to destroy us and we grow and learn from the challenging days we face, our destiny can be filled with fresh and new perspectives concerning life.

The year is 2006, and it has been eight years since I decided to change. The journey has been very difficult because I had to learn how to manage my money like never before.

If I didn't want to be broke, I needed to learn how to manage my money, because I could not just go hustle or make moves that would bring in some quick income anymore. Living check-to-check and not over-spending was one of the greatest lessons I had to learn. Learning to be content and the value of bargain shopping is priceless.

Focusing on money too much will drive you crazy. Someone said, "My favorite childhood memory? Not paying bills." Someone else said, "There's no way I was born to just pay bills and die." I could relate to these statements. In 2006, I had only enough money to pay the bills, and I remember crying out to God about how unfair life was. Here I was trying to live right. Trying to do the right thing. And it seemed like people who weren't living right had way more than I did.

I really wasn't doing all that bad. I had two cars, an old Caprice and a minivan. All my bills were paid on time. I lived on the good side of town in a two-bedroom apartment. I wasn't starving. I just didn't have a lot of money to buy things I didn't really need but just wanted.

After I was done crying about my life, I took time to reflect on how good my life really was compared to where I was headed before I decided to change. I wasn't locked up. I had been sober now for eight years, and my future was bright. So I decided to live a life of gratitude instead of complaining.

I tell people every day that when we wake up, there are two lists we can choose to think about. The first is those things we can be grateful for, like being able to hear, see, move our hands, feet, and mouth, and so much more we have to be thankful about. Or we can focus on the list to complain about. I have for years now decided to focus on the grateful list and trust God with what I think I have to complain about. The Word of God says, "Do all things without complaining and disputing" (Philippians 2:14).

It wasn't long after I changed my attitude that I received a raise and a promotion. I learned a valuable lesson at that point. *Just because something isn't happening for you right now doesn't mean that it will never happen.* You can't quit. Eventually you will reap what you sow. Success has no time limit. You will not become a successful person overnight. It takes time. But if you persist, good things will come. I am so glad I did not give up even though I wanted to so many times.

I know that money cannot buy happiness, but I seldom meet people who are broke who are happy. So please don't misunderstand what I am about to share with you. Because of the raise, I went from barely making it to being able to save over a thousand dollars a month, with much money to spare.

I was able to give away money if someone needed anything. I was able to pay for people's meals when we went out to eat. I bought a new car. I bought lots of guns. I moved from living in an apartment to purchasing my first home. I sold the Caprice and van and paid cash for an old-school 1978 Oldsmobile Ninety-Eight. I went to the store and paid cash for my rims.

I remember looking at my bank statement, and I had a little over $10,000 in my account. My life was good not because of the money or prosperity but because I knew then I had made the right decision in 1998 to change my life.

I have learned in life that you cannot hold on to what you have too tightly or with closed hands, you will never be able to receive what God has for you. The greatest man who ever lived said, "Take heed and beware of coveteousness, for one's life does not consist in the abundance of the things he possesses" (Luke 12:15).

So many believe their value is in what kind of clothes they wear, what kind of car they drive, or which neighborhood they live in. If that's true, your value would decrease every year as those things get older.

Our real worth comes from what kind of individual we are. This is why it's so important to never stop growing. What are you doing to make sure you keep growing mentally and spiritually? What are some areas where you can already see positive change in your life?

I am a happy man right now because what I have gained and the man I have become has far exceeded my expectations of what I had hoped for when I decided to change. As you continue to read my story, I know you will see that I made the right decision. It's a decision you can make too.

In chapter 13, I will show you how *outrageous* my thinking had become.

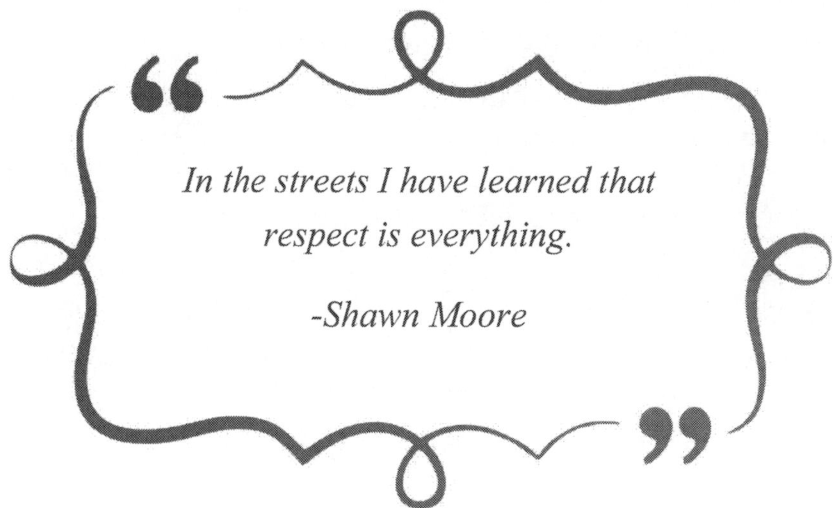
In the streets I have learned that
respect is everything.
-Shawn Moore

CHAPTER THIRTEEN

OUTRAGEOUS

It is around 1993, and I am twenty-three years old. One of my favorite things to do is to hang out at my friend's house smoking weed, with drugs in my pocket, guns nearby.

I remember one day looking around the room seeing a bunch of thugs and killers and saying to myself *nobody better mess with us right now*. It is a good feeling to have that kind of power and security to know that if something went down, we could and would take care of business.

One of my friends that I could count on was Panther. I loved talking to him. I remember one time I saw my friend Panther on Genessee Street, on the corner of Weber. So I'm pulling into the parking lot to talk to him when another car pulls up, and all I see is Panther's hand come out the window with his 9mm pointed at the guy in the other car. The guy pulls off fast, and Panther started to chase him, and I remember laughing and saying to myself, *Panther is crazy*. People used to mess with him because of his small stature, but in the streets, size doesn't matter, especially when you have a gun. I was grateful he was my friend and not my enemy.

In the late 80s, gangs were a big problem in Saginaw. My neighborhood was considered to be a small gang, but it was connected to every other gang in Saginaw. All of us knew somebody in the other gangs who was cool or else we were related somehow. It's crazy when you really think about what I just said.

I remember buying my first sawed-off shotgun from one of my boys who was in one of these other gangs we were connected to.

The more guns I accumulated, the safer I felt hanging around these guys. I felt like I was accepted by my friends, and at the time, I thought I needed that kind of acceptance.

So, nothing was better than being in a room with a bunch of crazy cats just like me. To feel like I was welcome somewhere and that someone loved me. I could do whatever and be whatever and say whatever, and people still respected and loved me just the way I was.

This particular night, we were doing what we do, sitting around with a house full of women and smoking weed, and I had just bought me a new gun. One of the biggest .38s you can find. It was nice and fat and bigger than some .357s.

I needed to go to the store and get some more blunts, but I was too high to take the gun with me, so I left it with two of my friends, Jaguar and Cheetah. Being so high, I knew that if I got pulled over, I would be searched. When we walked outside, I noticed three or four guys hanging outside about six houses down on the opposite side of the street. I didn't think much of it, so I left and went to the store alone.

When I came back, Jaguar hands me my gun, empty. Come to find out, those guys that we noticed were from a rival gang. They had a shootout while I was gone, and he used my gun. I'm sitting here thinking to myself every time something happens, I'm either at work, just leaving, or just pulling up. I was so upset, because I needed to earn stripes, and to earn stripes you have to put in work. So here I am disappointed because I wasn't involved in the shooting activities that my friends were so randomly and actively involved in.

Proverbs 23:17 says, "Do not let your heart envy sinners, but be zealous for the fear of the Lord all the day." I was wrong to desire to be known as a shooter. There is nothing honorable about being willing to take the life of another human being. God didn't design men to be killing each other. God didn't create us to die like that.

I don't believe I was just fortunate to be at the store at the time of the shootout, do you? In chapter 14, I will show you how *loyal* I was.

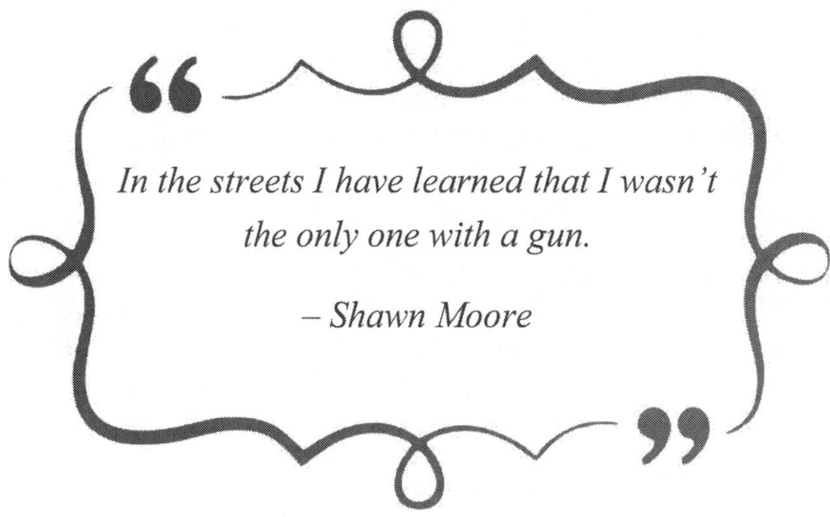
In the streets I have learned that I wasn't the only one with a gun.
– Shawn Moore

CHAPTER FOURTEEN

LOYAL

It's around 1995, and I am twenty-five years old. This night I was with my friend Cat, and we decided to go over to visit a girl he had been dating.

When we walked into her house, we saw it was full. There were nine gang members, some related to the girl Cat was dating. We went to school with about four of them, so we didn't think there was going to be any problems.

I quickly noticed most all of them were drunk and smoking weed. So we joined them in getting high, and one of them asked me where my gun was and what kind did I have. At the time I didn't think it was a strange question. I thought they were just trying to have conversation.

I told them I had a .38 and that I left it in my car. So now they knew I didn't have my gun on me. About four of them went outside, two of whom I knew from school, and I remember my car alarm went off, so I ran to the door. But they said one of them just bumped my car and the alarm went off. At the time I had no reason to doubt the story. But on the following day, I realized that someone had keyed my car, and it had to be one of them.

So we are getting high, and I overheard them talking about doing something to somebody. Cat and I were the only people in the house not in their clique. So I went into the living room, where Cat was with his girl, to tell him what I heard.

Cat was a wild and strong dude. He was always ready for a fight, and he knew how to fight. We decided that night Cat was going to be Booker T and I was Stevie Ray (better known as the wrestling tag team Harlem Heat).

At the private school, I had been in quite a few fights and had gotten pretty good with my hands, so I wasn't afraid, even though it was nine of them and only two of us. So I took off all my gold rings and was getting ready to hide my jewelry when all of them started to come into the living room with us. At the time, I was standing next to Cat, but I moved close to the door so we could spread the floor. One thing we thought was in our favor was they were drunk, sloppy drunk, and we hadn't drunk a thing.

While I am standing at the door, five or six of them surround Cat, and one of them pulls out a 9mm and starts pushing Cat's head with his finger. They were talking big junk about him messing with the girl he was dating. I guess she was dating one of them as well. The original plan was I would take four or five of them and he would handle the rest, but now they had surrounded him.

One of them that we had gone to school with looked at me and said "Bear," which was my street name, "you can leave. We only have a problem with Cat." Although I will always have mad love and respect for him giving me the opportunity to leave, I looked him in the face and told him that I wasn't leaving Cat there with them. I guess my man didn't realize how far Cat and I went back.

Cat was actually the one who gave me my street name. One day over at Python and Lion's house, we were getting high, and I grabbed Cat and held him tight. He said *get off me, you big bear*. It went from a joke to who I was. I tried to live as if I really was a bear. Have you ever seen anyone running up on a bear without a gun? Not a wise decision. So it was nothing for me to say *we came here together, and we were leaving together*.

At that moment, I made eye contact with Cat, and I could see it in his eyes that he was about to rush the one with the gun, which wasn't a good idea. I shook my head side to side to say *no*. I am glad he listened to me, because all they did was threaten him and push his head with their finger. Cat was a crazy dude, and if he would have done what he wanted to do, who knows what the outcome would have been for us. After they warned him, they ran through the house yelling and screaming *don't mess with us*, and then they left.

I remember being so mad when we left that house! I was thinking that when we got back to the hood, it was on. But a good part of my crew was like, we don't want no trouble, because we went to school with these guys. Only a few of my friends were ready to ride, and most of them were not my friends from the neighborhood. This hurt me bad, because I thought we were like family. Sometimes we expect more from others because we would be willing to do that much for them.

I learned a valuable lesson that night. If something really went down, I had to be prepared to do my dirt by myself if I had to. Proverbs 25:19 says, "Confidence in an unfaithful man in time of trouble is like a bad tooth and a foot out of joint."

I don't believe it's a coincidence that I walked out of that house alive that night, do you? Or that no one in my immediate crew wanted to do anything about the incident. But in chapter 15, I will show you how I was *betrayed.*

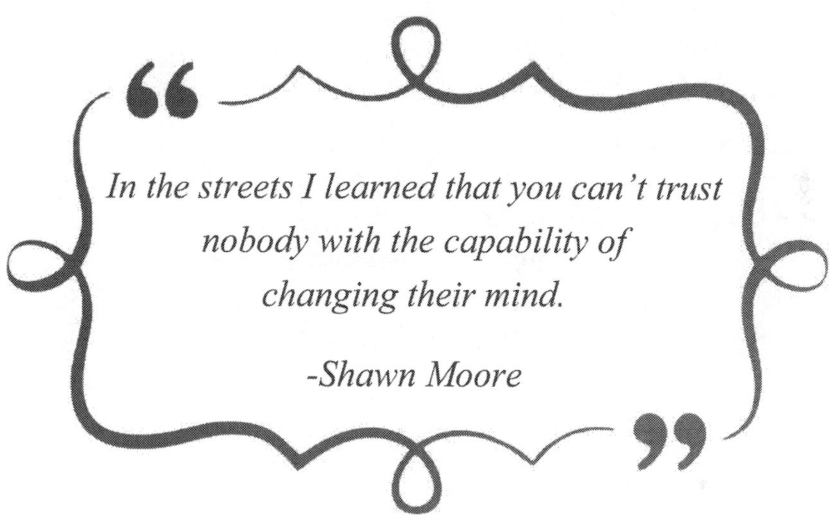
In the streets I learned that you can't trust nobody with the capability of changing their mind.
-Shawn Moore

CHAPTER FIFTEEN

BETRAYAL

The saddest thing about betrayal is that it doesn't come from your enemies but from those close to you. It was roughly 1996, and I was twenty-six years old and looking forward to hanging out with my good friend Snake.

Snake was my guy. There was an incident when someone had broken into my family's shed and stolen our lawn mower. Snake was right there, initiating my dad and I chasing the man around our neighborhood and getting our lawn mower back. Snake rode to school with me every day, and whenever I had problems in the streets, Snake was one of the few people I could count on to have my back. He was always ready for whatever.

Snake had my back regardless of how many or who it was. My enemies were his enemies, and vice versa. Whenever Snake would hook up with a girl, he would hook me up with her friend. Real talk, it would take an entire different book to tell you all that Snake and I have been through together. Truthfully, most of it I would refuse to talk about.

This day, I arrived at Snake's house, and Cat was there as well. Snake told me he wanted to drive, which was odd. Whenever Snake and I hung out, I was always the one behind the wheel. Then Snake said something even more strange: he asked me not to bring my gun! I had never heard him make such a request in my life. Snake had more people that didn't like him than I did.

At the time, I was wearing over $3,000 dollars in jewelry, with over $4,000 of dope in my pockets, and I had at least $2,000 in cash on me. And since I had all that money, I didn't care for the idea of not having my gun on me. Snake and I argued about this for fifteen minutes, but I finally gave in to him. He said he didn't feel right having the gun in the car. I said okay, if that's how you feel, I will leave my gun at home.

We headed to a night club, and Snake says he needs to make a stop first. We go straight to a strange neighborhood, and I didn't feel safe at all. I started asking question about who lives here, how long are we going to be here, and what are we doing here in the first place?

Snake tried to reassure me and said we wouldn't be long at all. We were just sitting at this strange house, for apparently no reason (or as he said, he was meeting someone), and I got mad. I kept thinking I shouldn't have listened to Snake and left my gun behind. We just sat there for about thirty minutes. We rolled up a joint in the time that we were waiting, but we really couldn't enjoy getting high not knowing where we were. And I could tell Snake was in no hurry to leave. But eventually, we did.

In Proverbs 27:5–6, the author says, "Open rebuke is better than love carefully concealed. Faithful are the wounds of a friend, but the kisses of an enemy are deceitful." It's a cold world, and being blind to the fact that everybody that is close to you don't have your best interest is just unwise.

Snake, Cat, and I finally made it to the club and had a good time. We left the club about 1 in the morning, and I was ready to go.

While we are driving home, my pager goes off, and it's Cobra. I ask Snake to pull over so I could use a pay phone. While on the phone, Gorilla pulls up and jumps out of his car with a .357 magnum and stands about ten feet away from me. I have no idea what to do since I don't have a gun on me. As Gorilla was coming toward me, I told Cobra what was happening and to call the police. Then I just stayed on the phone as if was I was talking, and Gorilla just stood there staring at me.

Cat jumps out of the car and tries to talk to Gorilla, and another car pulls up. This third car is one of our homegirls from the neighborhood. I hang up the phone and go over to her car to give her my jewelry, my money, and the drugs I had in my pocket. I told her to leave and I would call her later to get my stuff. Then I got into the car with Snake and asked him why he was just sitting there and not talking to Gorilla since he had made me leave my gun at home. Gorilla and Snake were cool. I only knew Gorilla through Snake. But before Snake could respond, the parking lot swarmed with police.

Gorilla took off running, and the police didn't even bother to chase him. They questioned Snake, Cat, and me because when Cobra called the police, he told them someone was being robbed, and they automatically assumed it was the store. When they realized it was just us in the parking lot and nothing happening in the store, you could see them quickly lose interest in the situation.

After the police left, the three of us drove back to the hood so that I could get my stuff from our homegirl, but what I really wanted was to get my gun. Our girl met us at Snake's house, and while we're telling her what happened, the phone rang. It was Gorilla. I wasn't that surprised that he wasn't caught by the police.

Snake was talking to him, but I took the phone and told Gorilla that I hoped he was ready to do what he had to when the time came. I was letting him know he'd better be ready to shoot after messing around with me. Gorilla said he was, and he didn't care. I asked him why he didn't do anything but just stand there staring at me, and his response almost floored me. Gorilla said he didn't do anything because he wasn't sure that Snake had kept his end of the deal by making sure I didn't have a gun on me.

I didn't want to believe Gorilla, but I knew it was true, because Snake had never asked me to leave my gun before. I don't know why Snake was setting me up. I assume it was because I was getting money and didn't put him on. I never asked him why. In fact, I never told him I knew about it. I just handed the phone back to Snake and didn't say a word about it.

I was once again reminded that I couldn't trust anyone, not even someone I thought was a good friend. The writer of Psalms 118:8 says, "It is better to trust in the Lord than to put confidence in man." With this happening to me, I was once again reminded how true this is.

Even so, Snake was more beneficial to me as a friend that I couldn't trust than as an enemy. There was no way I was going to push Snake out of my life.

I kept him close until the day he was murdered. We actually talked two weeks before he died. He was so excited about his new girlfriend and wanted me to meet her real bad, but I was living out of town at the time. I made it home for his funeral. That's what big homies do, we stay true to the end, and even in the streets we can forgive and show love to someone others may say doesn't deserve it.

Truthfully, everyone in the streets shows love to someone at one time or another who others say doesn't deserve it. We only have a short time to love. This is why it's so important not to let what others think about you dictate your decisions. Only a few of my homies knew what he tried to do to me, but I never treated him differently. However, from that point on, whenever I went out with Snake, I always drove.

Snake played a big part in why I started carrying more than one gun. Every time I bought a new gun, I would go straight to his house and show it to him. He would say that I was crazy and ask what was going on. I would tell him I didn't know who I could trust, and I wasn't going to let someone else take my life.

As much as I wanted to believe that statement, I have heard of and know of some real street cats that have died from being shot. The truth of the matter is that no one is in control of when they die. When it's your time, it's your time. However, it's humbling to know that your life can be over real quick due to guns being in the hand of someone who is not mature and responsible enough to have one. This is not the way the Creator designed for us to die.

A lack of love is one of the biggest problems in our streets and in the world today. We have so many young people in jail today for killing people before they assess a situation. Yes, it is a challenge to love someone who has betrayed you. I can tell you from experience that while it's hard, it is possible. Life was going to be a challenge for me no matter which choice I made with Snake. I decided to take the path of love and forgiveness.

I never found out why he betrayed me. To me, it really didn't matter. He was my boy for life. At the same time, I knew I couldn't trust him.

Having a friend like Snake taught me what Scarface said about who do I trust? Me! That's who! For real. However, over my years of being sober, I have learned that I can't even trust myself. Sometimes I find myself doing things I don't want to do and the things I should do I can't find the strength to do (See Paul's letter to the Romans, chapter 7, verses 15–20). So for me, I have learned the only person I can truly trust is God!

It's not a coincidence that I wasn't shot or robbed or worse the night Snake betrayed me. In chapter 16, I will show you how I was *protected* from harm.

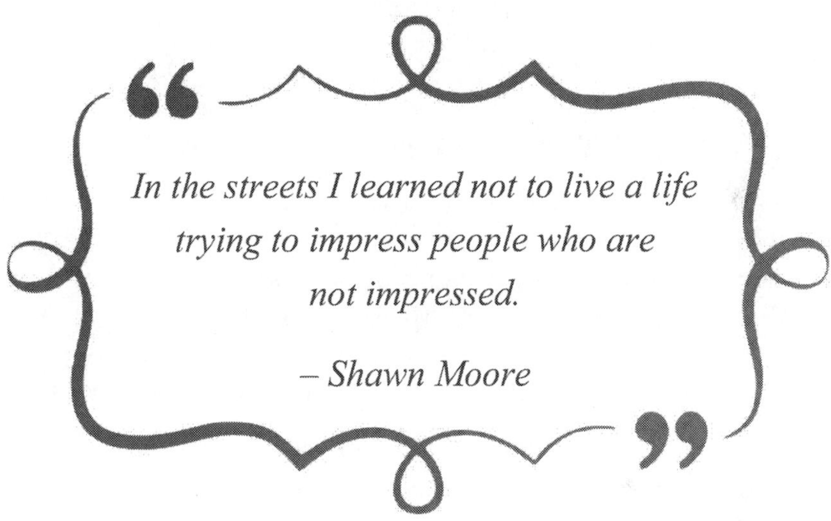
In the streets I learned not to live a life trying to impress people who are not impressed.
– Shawn Moore

CHAPTER SIXTEEN

PROTECTED

It was close to 1988, and I was eighteen years old. A car pulls up beside me as I am arriving at school one morning. The driver asked if I was Shawn Moore. I said yes, and he just drove away.

That made me nervous and afraid of what was about to happen. There was a lot of gang activity during that time, and people were getting shot frequently.

I did some detective work by using what car he was driving to find out who he was. So I decided to confront him and find out if there was a problem. He accused me of talking about his sister, but I had no idea what he was talking about as I didn't really know his sister or anything about her. I thought everything was cool after I talked to him, but I wasn't sure.

Later that night, I was hanging out on Genessee Street, the strip, which was about a mile or two long. Every weekend we would park in the lots of the local businesses up and down the street. The street would be packed with cars driving back and forth. It was the place to see and be seen.

My cousin Teddy loved Genessee Street. If I wanted to find him, I just had to drive up and down, and eventually I'd run into him. So that day, some friends of mine—Snake, Buffalo, and Wolf, along with five others and myself—were hanging with Teddy in the parking lot across from the car wash. And then the same dude I had confronted earlier pulled up and jumped out the car with three of his friends.

I had already told my cousin and friends what had happened that morning, and it turned out that Teddy knew the guy. Teddy runs up on him, and they talk. When they finished, the dude came over to me, gave me a hug, and we talked. I told him again it was a misunderstanding since I didn't know his sister. He turned out to be a cool dude, and we have remained cordial toward one another to this day.

That night on the strip, I wasn't too worried about the situation since we were about ten deep, including Snake, Wolf, and Buffalo. I remember the first time I met Wolf, which was at the private school I had attended. Wolf was involved in the street from a young age, and the leaders of this school were trying to help him by finding sponsors to pay tuition for him to attend the private school. Wolf had killers in his family, and he wasn't far from becoming one himself.

Wolf told the leaders at the school that he had enemies, but I don't think they believed him at first. But that changed after they sent him out into the neighborhood to invite people to church. He came back with bullet holes in the car and the window shot out.

Wolf was the real deal. His family was in and out of jail. Since there weren't too many black students at the private school, he and I connected and became good friends.

While we were at that school, some people thought that he was taking my lunch from me, but in reality, I was sharing it with him, even though he aggressively asked me for it. My parents always blessed me with more food in my lunch than I could eat, so I shared it with Wolf.

During that time, Wolf knew that I didn't know a lot about the streets, so he was willing to protect me at school. Wolf wasn't going to let anyone do anything to me, and that made me feel strong and safe. At the time I was shy and I had a fear of street people, but having Wolf around helped me lose that fear, because I knew he had my back.

Buffalo and I also met at the same private school, and he was the real deal, just like Wolf. Having a crew that included Wolf and Buffalo made me feel as if I was a part of something. We watched out for each other.

For example, we were all three in Bay City, which is predominantly a white area, and it was clear we were not welcome. Wolf was having problems with a guy over some girls. So it was nothing for me to tell that guy and his friends not to make me pop my trunk. You see, in Bay City, black men got pulled over all the time, so I kept my guns in the trunk.

When I said that, they just left. To this day, Wolf reminds me about that incident and what I did for him, but it was like that in the streets. One day someone has your back, and the next day you had theirs. Proverbs 20:6 says, "Most men will proclaim each his own goodness, but who can find a faithful man?" I had a few faithful friends in my life, and I am thankful for them. Do you have any faithful friends in your life? Is there anyone who would count you as one of their faithful friends?

Anyway, that night on the strip, I knew that Snake, Buffalo, and Wolf would have my back, as well as my cousin Teddy and my other friends. Even so, it was not simply luck or a coincidence that Teddy knew that dude and was able to squash any issue before it came to me. Yet, in chapter 17, I will show you how someone in my *family* almost got me into some trouble.

In the streets I learned that if I'm willing to die for something, it should be for my family, not for a neighborhood that we don't even own.

– Shawn Moore

CHAPTER SEVENTEEN

FAMILY

It's probably 1990, and I am twenty-one years old and had been working second shift at Arby's, getting off work between 11 and 12 at night. One day, I was trying to sleep in when the phone rang.

It was my little sister, and she was whispering. I knew she was at school, so I'm wondering what's up. She was in the twelfth grade at this time, only eighteen years old. She told me this guy said he was going to slap her because of our cousin who affiliated with a gang that he had issues with. In Proverbs 21:23, the author says, "Whoever guards his mouth and tongue keeps his soul from troubles." People really need to stop and think before they speak. I guess he didn't realize how much I loved my family, especially my little sister.

I jumped out of bed, got dressed, and drove to my old high school, where she met me at the door. We went to this guy's class and knocked on the door. I was just going to let him know not to threaten my sister when I felt a hand on my shoulder and heard a voice say, "You don't want to do that." It was the school principal, who was one of my former teachers when I attended there.

He escorted us to his office, where I explained the situation. He said it was best for me to let him handle it. I left, but I went to get Snake and Cat. We came back to the school around lunchtime and drove through the parking lot to let the guy know I was there. Everyone that was outside saw us, and I was truthfully just trying to scare him. I knew I couldn't really do anything while he was at school without going to jail. Gossip spreads quickly, plus the principal had probably already spoken to him. I also wanted him to know I was not going to take anyone threatening my little sister and not do anything about it.

About a week later, I saw him riding on Genessee Street. Snake was with me, and I hit a U-turn to pull up beside him. I looked him directly in the eyes and asked him if he wanted to see me. He looked at me and said no. He could tell that I wasn't playing about my little sister. His response made me feel really good that he had enough respect (or fear) for me and my reputation that he didn't want any trouble. Sure, he was only one person and just a kid in school, and I knew that we still had a lot of work to do to earn our respect from the entire city, but even so, I felt good.

When I got home that night, my sister was on the phone with a friend of mine who lived around the corner from us. He told her to tell me that there was this guy at his house who said he didn't like me. Without thinking, I get in my car and drive around the corner to my friend's place to check this guy as well. I'm feeling pretty good about myself at this point. When I get there, this guy comes outside and says, "Nobody messing with you man. You probably got a gun on you." I looked at him and told him I did but he was the one saying he didn't like me.

Now, at this point, I'm being foolish. This guy could've shot me. If he had just started shooting, there wasn't really anything I could've done about it, because I didn't have my finger on the trigger.

As far as I know, he didn't have a gun. But the point I am trying to make is that he could have had a gun. All I was thinking was that I had to go check this guy because he said he didn't like me. He had tried me a few times throughout the years, so I don't think he was afraid of me.

Probably the only thing that saved me on this night was that he knew I most likely had a gun on me. What he didn't know is whether I would use it.

My man and I are cordial to this day. Proverbs 16:32 says, "He who is slow to anger is better than the mighty, and he who rules his spirit than he who takes a city." It's a good thing to not let your emotions get the best of you. This is one of those times I could have been in real trouble because I was so quick to get angry.

It was not luck or a coincidence that I didn't get myself killed while I was running up on people trying to earn respect in the streets. I used the same tactics on many more people, and it worked all the time. Most of them wouldn't try to be hard if caught alone without their homies.

People like to act harder than they really are when there is a crowd around. I didn't give people that chance. I was into one-on-one or that face-to-face business with those who didn't like me. If there was a problem, I was trying to resolve it as quickly as possible before it escalated. My life was really about making money, not killing people. However, I felt I was willing to do that if I had to.

In chapter 18, I will show you how *foolish* I had become with carrying a gun.

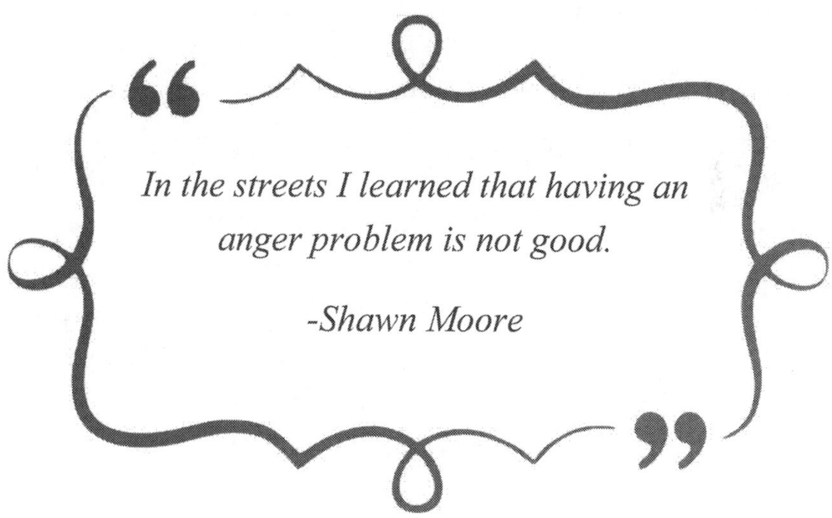
In the streets I learned that having an anger problem is not good.
-Shawn Moore

CHAPTER EIGHTEEN

FOOLISH

At the private Christian school I attended, black kids were always coming and going. I was one of the few that attended consistently for years. Actually, I went there for about eight years, all the way to the twelfth grade, when I got myself kicked out.

Alligator was one of the young black kids that attended for a little while. We were good friends until he moved away and I lost contact with him. But before I tell you about Alligator, I have to tell you about Cheetah.

Cheetah and I were hanging out on Bay Road at Stardust, which was a bowling alley and bar. It was risky hanging on Bay Road, because the police in that area did not play. Everyone knew you could go to jail in a hurry hanging out there, and it's still that way to this day.

Both Cheetah and I carried guns, and Cheetah was well-known and respected. We're having a good time doing what we do—playing pool and spending time with the ladies. We were both drunk and high, and the place was about to close.

Just as we're leaving the parking lot, the police pull us over. My heart is racing, because I have drugs on me, and we both have guns. I'm so drunk and high that I can't walk without staggering.

I ask the officer what's going on, and he says they are looking for some guy that was involved in a fight. The guy had the same first name as Cheetah. The officer took our IDs and ran the license plates. When he came back to the car, he told us to drive safe. I was shocked! He didn't ask to search the vehicle, and he had to know we were drunk and/or high, and yet, he didn't do anything. I just knew we were both going to jail, but it didn't happen.

Now, keep that incident in mind while I tell you about Alligator. After losing contact with Alligator for several years, I somehow got back in touch. I think his sister and mine ended up talking to each other, which allowed Alligator and I to reconnect. He was living in Seattle, Washington, but was returning to Saginaw to visit his dad, who still lived in the area.

So we got together, and I learned that Alligator also smoked weed. We left to go get some and got high. His cousin came over, and we went for a ride.

While we were out riding around, the police pulled up behind us. There's smoke coming out the windows of the car, but we quickly put out the joint. We figure we're about to be pulled over. Everyone knew that if more than two black men were in the car, the possibility of getting pulled over rose dramatically. I also had a gun on me, so I just knew that we were going to jail.

The car smelled like weed, and if the police had pulled us over, he would have gotten a contact as soon as he got out of his patrol car. To my surprise, the officer followed us for about three miles but never pulled us over. I think he just wanted to make us sweat.

Well, the plan worked. I was wet all over, and my heart was pounding as hard as if I was in the ocean and saw the fin of a shark.

We headed to Tiger's house to continue smoking weed. Now, Tiger's house was the place to be. Not only was it permissible to smoke weed there, but people came to Tiger's house all through the day and night. I wanted to show Alligator and his cousin a good time, and Tiger's house was the place to hang out, because women were always over there.

One of my friends, Crocodile, was also at Tiger's, and he was being disrespectful. I can't remember exactly what he said, but it was inappropriate. I hadn't seen Alligator in years, and I couldn't let him think I was a punk with Crocodile disrespecting me like that. So I hit Crocodile in the mouth and told him to shut up. Actually, I sucker punched him in front of a house full of people. I was so determined to get my respect that I acted without thinking. But honestly, I didn't do that to everyone who I felt disrespected me. I just wanted to make a point.

I remember having a bad temper and problems controlling my anger. I can remember when my thoughts went from beating up people to killing them. I would see myself killing someone by shooting them directly in the face multiple times. I would visualize myself standing over them and emptying the clip into their body. I would think about killing their entire family. I thought I was losing my mind from having such messed up thoughts.

I am thankful that Crocodile didn't challenge me that day, because I did have a gun on me. Hitting him like that broke one of the personal rules I had for myself. That rule was that I was no longer going to fight or put my hands on anyone. This became a rule for me because too many were losing their lives in physical altercations. Therefore, I viewed it as a waste of time to beat someone up when that might just allow them to go get their friends and family and then come back with a gun.

My philosophy instead was to talk it out, to reconcile and seek peace. The only other alternative was to start with the guns. But this time, I didn't even try to talk to Crocodile. I let my emotions get the best of me, and I hit him. Proverbs 14:17 says, "A quick-tempered man acts foolishly, and a man of wicked intentions is hated."

Getting angry quick put me in some messed up situations at times. Thankfully, Crocodile didn't let his emotions get the best of him. He let it pass. But then and now, there is (usually) no forgiveness in the streets.

Three different scenarios and each time, I'm able to walk away without going to jail or getting shot. It was not a coincidence. I told you about the story with Cheetah first so you can see how foolish

I was living, yet I am not getting caught up like everyone else. At the time I didn't understand it. I thought I was just lucky or street-smart. But in the last chapter I am going to share with you what I believe was really going on.

In chapter 19, I will show you how *insane* my life was becoming.

In the streets I learned that you better have a day that you take a look in the mirror and do a true assessment of the decisions you are making.

– Shawn Moore

CHAPTER NINTEEN

INSANE

Months have passed since the judge had sentenced me to 25 years to life. I knew it was wrong to kill people, but that is just part of the lifestyle I had decided to live. Now it's time for me to suffer the consequences for the choices I had made.

In the 80s, everyone wanted to be a rapper. Some of my friends were a part of this rap group in Saginaw called TCT. I never told them, but I wanted to be a guest on a song with them. So I started working on my rap skills and wrote a few songs and hooks.

One song I wrote was called "Hook You Up Like Cable." However, I knew I was in trouble when I wrote the song called: "Who Want to Die Today?"

I started singing to myself in the mirror with my guns in my hand. This song I had written went like this:

Who want to die today?

You? Oh I can help you with that

Won't be no shooting you in your back

Let me get my gat

Oh you hungry

Eat these bullets in your mouth n----

How do they taste

You want how many n----

3,4,5,6 to your face

Someone should have taught you how to act n----

Now ain't no coming back n----

I know you didn't expect to see me standing over your body

Now you're saying to yourself I didn't know he had ambition like John Gotti

It's too late to apologize now

Go slow, who want to die today?

Who want to die today?

Blank your crew, your family too

I don't care what your uncles and cousins use to do

That includes your momma and daddy too

I got enough room for all their bodies in the back of my caddy

Oh you didn't see the sign: Beware of Bears

It's that n---- named Oso who will kill you slowly with a pillow

Oh that's not working let me put my gun next to it

Let me squeeze the trigger, aw that's better

Time to get this cheddar

Money, bread, whatever you call it

That what I said

2 the head n----

Now you dead n----

Who want to die today? Who want to die today?

It's 1997, and my life is filled with anger. I ask myself is it okay for me to just start killing people. In my mind, it was, but I couldn't stop thinking about my parents, especially my mother.

My mom and I were really close, and I knew how much she loved me. She was a cancer survivor, and the last thing I wanted to do was to hurt her. Most young people like myself don't think about the immense stress and worry we put on the family member who is concerned about our safety and well-being.

Gun violence doesn't just hurt the one murdered. It hurts the family, community, and God. In some cases, unwise decisions can put a financial strain on the family, because they're trying to pay for a lawyer or constantly putting money in someone's commissary account unnecessarily, all because of a bad decision. GoFundMe accounts are so popular today for those who die young with no life insurance. It only makes sense for someone who is not living right to think about someone else other than themselves. That is exactly what I decided to do.

All I could see in my head was my mom coming to visit me in prison and saying *you couldn't do better than this with your life?* For a few days I replayed that scene several times in my head. There are a bunch of real street cats that can relate to what I am talking about. I didn't really want to just take a man's life, but for some really foolish reasons, I was willing to. Only someone ignorant of the game would say somebody's not hard, or is soft, just because they refused to pull the trigger in certain situations. Nobody has pulled the trigger every single time the opportunity has presented itself.

Some don't think, but some do. I just happen to be a thinker. It doesn't make you a coward to consider the consequences of your decisions. It is a wise person who considers the consequences of what they choose to do. Many have made decisions and wished they could take it back.

Ask yourself, are you a thinker, or do you just react? Anyone who can take the life of someone else without thinking about it needs some help mentally and spiritually. You can't just take a life when you fear God. Mature people know how to resolve conflict without using a gun. Immature people lack communication skills and therefore resort to violence. I thought about how my parents were God-fearing people and faithful in church. I saw how good their life was compared to mine.

My dad was a man. I knew he would be hurt, but he would have done what men do. He would have adjusted, but not my mom. She would have been devastated.

I thank God for the foundation that was laid in my life. If it wasn't for that foundation, I would have been in trouble, like a lot of my friends. I would not have known that I can pray to God. I am a living witness that God hears our prayers. When we are willing to put in the work, he can change our lives. So today, I am grateful to say that the beginning of this chapter could have been my story, but it isn't. No judge has ever sentenced me to twenty-five years or life in prison. However, that would or could have been my story if I hadn't decided I needed to change.

And then I actually did change.

I believe God gives everyone a chance to change the course of their lives. Most of the time, people are too high or drunk to see the chance. Fortunately for me, I was so angry for a while that I didn't feel like getting high. So I knew if I was going to avoid going to prison, this was my only chance.

I started praying to see if God was real or not. I didn't know if He could help me. My prayer went like this. "God, if You can hear me, if You are real, I need Your help right now."

I am about to do something really stupid, and I can't stop myself. It's like it's already done. The handwriting is already on the wall. This was my destiny: to be a killer. I had been living for this moment, and the time had finally come for me to really kill someone. I always thought it would happen, and it was just my time. I said, "God, if You can take this anger away from me, if there is a possibility for me to do something different, please help me. Because the thoughts I am having right now are insane."

To my surprise, God sent a man of God to my house, similar to how you came across this book somehow. I didn't understand what God was doing at first. However, I started learning He wanted me to trust Him and live life His way and not like I had been doing. God, through the preaching of His Word, gave me victory over anger, alcoholism, philandering, drug abuse, cursing, and lusting. And He is still working on and in me to this day.

I don't believe it is a coincidence that I am not locked up or dead. The only reason I shared all these stories with you is so you can see the type of person that I was and the people I was hanging around.

It's amazing that I am the man that I am today compared to what I used to be. This wasn't just a few incidents or a few bad decisions that I made. This was my lifestyle. The street life. But that life wasn't taking me where I wanted to go.

I no longer live life merely surviving. I have the opportunity now to invest in others.

Please don't misunderstand me. What I have been able to accomplish is not easy. It is a challenge to leave the street life. It's not easy to live life sober and deal with people. There have been so many who have tried to get out of the street life only to fail.

But we have too many good kids falling victim to these streets. So many are born into this environment and find it hard to escape. Yes, the task is laborious, but it's not impossible.

If I can change, anybody can change.

We have a widespread outbreak of violence that needs to stop. If we desire to see a decrease in violence, we must deal with the real problem. The real problem we have today is not guns but people. People do not want to change, and I get it, because change is hard.

Change was hard for me too. I had to change my routine. I went from getting up thinking about money, women, and getting lit to waking up thinking about God, the purpose of my life, and how I was going to position myself to help others. I decided to spend time with mature working men instead of people who didn't see the value in working hard to provide for their families and pursue their dreams. This wasn't easy at first. But it sure paid off in the long run.

Who you spend your time with will dictate your future. Proverbs 13:20 says, "He who walks with wise men will be wise, but the companion of fools will be destroyed." It's my desire now to challenge young people to come and walk with me. Let me show you something different. I have been blessed to be able to teach the youth and adults that change is possible if we believe. I made a choice to change. The decision was challenging, but now I am so grateful for it.

Please don't get it twisted. There are many stories that I did not put in this book and that I refuse to talk about. I have only given you a glimpse of what I've been through—moments and choices that could have changed the course of my life forever. I don't think it's fair for me to live the life that I am living while the world is the way it is today. We have too many young people dying in these streets and way too many locked up or headed in that direction.

In chapter 20, I will share with you what triggered my desire to decide its time to change.

In the streets I've learned that one of the greatest decisions a man or a woman can make in their lifetime is to never stop growing as an individual.

– Shawn Moore

CHAPTER TWENTY

CHANGE

The world we live in today is very ***dangerous*** and we are faced with tough decisions daily. Every day we make ***decisions*** about when to get up, what to wear, what to eat, where to go, what to do, where to live, and much more. We make decisions that are ***dumb***, ***crazy***, or even ***illogical***. We take ***chances*** we should not take. We do things we should not do.

Each decision we make comes with ***real*** consequences. Being on time makes others view you as ***reliable***. Wearing a tuxedo to a pool party makes others view you as ***ridiculous***. What we hold ***close*** to our hearts or who we consider as ***friends*** influences our decisions. The decisions of others affect us too.

The world you live in may leave with you without ***hope*** because of the ***outrageous*** things happening around you. You may think no one is ***loyal*** because you see ***betrayal*** too many times. How can you feel safe and ***protected*** when your own ***family*** often lets you down because of ***foolish*** decisions? It can all drive you ***insane***!

If that is how you are feeling—lost, desperate, and alone—then it is time for a ***change***. Regardless of your circumstances, despite what you have done and what you see around you. Change is possible if only you make the decision to ***believe***.

Transformations do happen. I have been transformed for the last twenty-five years, but the life that I am living today is not just for me.

I recently took a class in CPR—cardiopulmonary resuscitation (how to save someone's life when they can't breathe). The instructor told us how the American Heart Association had made a decision to change how CPR was administered. In 2008, the AHA released new recommendations that say bystanders can skip mouth-to-mouth resuscitation and use hands-only CPT to help an adult who suddenly collapses. In hand-only CPR, bystanders did not have to be concerned with mouth-to-mouth CPR. That one decision has improved the success rate in saving lives.

Right now, everyone is talking about black lives matter and stop the violence, but no one is willing to address the real issue. The real issue in our world today is that no one wants to take a long look in the mirror.

One of my kids drools when they sleep. I can always tell when they haven't looked in the mirror. I ask, "You didn't look in the mirror, did you?" "How did you know?" "Your face is dirty, slobber everywhere." The same is true in life. People are okay with their lifestyle being dirty because they refuse to take a look in the mirror. Others can see it, but you're okay with it.

Until I was honest about who I was, nothing changed in my life. I am challenging people to do what I did in 1998. I asked myself, *where is your life headed if you keep doing what you are doing?* I didn't like the answer and decided I wanted to do something different. I am amazed at how my life has turned out compared to others who refuse to take a look in the mirror.

The moment we step foot on a car lot, we know the car salesman, at the end of the day, is only concerned about selling us a car. He is interested in how much money he can get us to spend on a car. That doesn't stop us from buying cars. After you have a car for a few years, everyone knows that eventually we will experience car troubles. Now we must deal with a mechanic. It's hard to find a mechanic you can trust. That doesn't stop us from buying cars, because we see the value of having a car.

It amazes me how many people say they don't want anything to do with church because all the pastor wants is your money. That may be true in some churches, but we need to treat pastors and churches like we do mechanics and car salesmen. Keep looking until you find a good one.

I have prayed for you to see how important it is to have a personal relationship with God. I don't believe in coincidences. I am not saying if you go to church, you can't die young or get locked up. However, the odds are definitely against you if you are not making wise decisions. A real man of God teaching the Word of God accurately should help us to make better choices. Don't misunderstand me. I know the church is not perfect, but neither is the world we live in.

One of the core teachings in the church is love. Right now, the world and the church need to learn a lot more about this single subject. A life without God involved can be frustrating, disappointing, empty, lonely, and oftentimes ineffective.

I was twenty-eight years old when I decided to change. It's never too late to do something different with your life. Ultimately, the decision is yours, but I have to say that my life has been much better with God involved.

What about your life? Don't let people hinder you from having a relationship with God. Don't believe that you can have a close relationship with God and not go to church.

Just like the NBA and NFL are hiring former players to be analysts because they played and understand the game and can speak from experience and a different viewpoint, we need to stop looking for people who have never been in the streets or fake people who claim to be street to help us solve the violence that plagues our nation. If we want real change, we better start listening to the people who have lived that life and have already changed.

We need to rebuke those who are profiting and benefiting from promoting and glamorizing the ways of the street, camouflaging themselves as changed individuals.

It was Jesus who saved my life. People live their entire lives trying to fit in and be accepted by their peers and society. One thing I learned about the world is you have to be a certain way for everyone to accept you. So why do people get mad at God for having expectations for us to truly have a relationship with Him? Everyone else is the same way, yet the benefits of knowing God outweigh any earthly relationship we can experience.

I don't care how many or how big the mistakes you have made. There is hope for you if you put your trust in God. Real hope can only come from knowing God through repentance and salvation. When you start living according to God's purpose nothing will be the same.

In chapter 21, I will highlight the first seven things (out of fourteen) that I did to help me change my life.

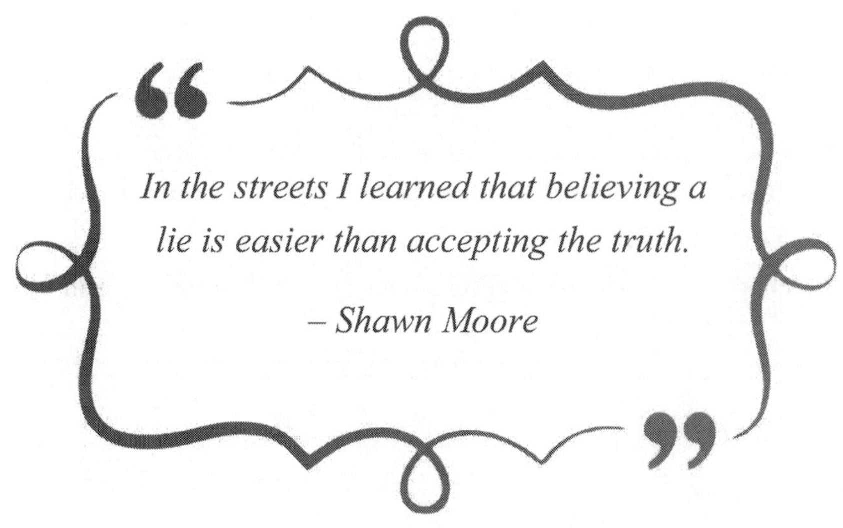
In the streets I learned that believing a lie is easier than accepting the truth.
– Shawn Moore

CHAPTER TWENTY ONE

BELIEVE

In the 90s, I watched the movies *Colors*, *Scarface*, *American Me*, *Carlito's Way*, *King of New York*, *New Jack City*, *Boys in the Hood*, *Blood in Blood Out*, *Menace to Society*, *A Bronx Tale*, and *South Central* almost monthly. However, I wasn't just watching these movies for entertainment. I was taking notes. Most of the time in the movies and in the streets, the one on top always ended up dead or locked up in the end. I didn't want that to be my story. So I decided to believe instead of doubting. I am no longer a street person because I believed I didn't have to be.

Change is not easy. It will require hard work and determination, but it is possible. Here is what I did.

1. I decided to find several mentors and trusted their advice even when I didn't understand or necessarily agree. What I learned right away was that my mentors were not perfect. But I intentionally looked past their flaws and learned from them anyway. It is not just athletes that need a little coaching. Everyone needs practical advice from someone with more experience, because we don't know everything.

I would highly recommend that you never stop listening to someone who is pushing you to grow as an individual. Learn from people you admire and those who are doing something positive with their life. If you are broke or close to it and your mentor isn't, you probably need to listen to their advice. It's funny to me how people are so immature and prideful that they refuse to listen to people who are doing better than they are.

2. I decided to fight my way through failure, because I did mess up sometimes. When you fail, be honest with yourself, other people, and most definitely, God. It would be nice if everyone was persistent or relentless and never needed to start over or ask for forgiveness, but that ain't real life. One thing I learned is that failing is a part of life. Have a plan of what to do next any time you fail. Don't quit, and don't give up. Keep starting over if you have to. We only fail when we stop trying. I decided not to let my failures be the end of my story.

3. I decided to quickly forget whatever negative things people said to me or about me. I've learned that if I can't forget it, I can use it as motivation to succeed. Having negative people in your life can destroy you or accelerate you toward your destiny. Dealing with negative people will tell you something about yourself. It forced me to grow and to examine myself about how badly I really wanted to change. So many pointed out my flaws, but because I didn't quit, today I am an overcomer, not a victim. I do way more today that pleases God than I do that displeases him.

4. I decided not to quit even though I wanted to quit a thousand times. We must learn to finish what we start. So many give up way too soon. We cannot depend on others to encourage us all the time. Having a vision will help keep us focused on the goal. We must learn to live with passion. If you struggle with passion, pray for God to give you hope and focus. Surround yourself with people who will remind you not to quit.

NFL coach Vince Lombardi once said, "Winners never quit, and quitters never win." This quote is on the wall in my office. Successful speaker and author Brian Tracy has stated, "Obstacles are what you see when you take your eyes off your goals." I decided to have tunnel vision, with zero tolerance for anything not pushing me toward being a better man.

5. I decided to be a faithful man. You can't be called faithful if you are constantly unfocused on where you want to be in life. To become this faithful man, I learned to consistently discipline myself to do the hard things that I really didn't want to do, and to

do them *right now.* For instance, reading is hard for me, but I consistently read every day. Taking constructive criticism is hard for me when the person who is giving the criticism isn't humble or perfect. However, over the years I have consistently taken criticism (advice) from people I thought needed to take a look in the mirror themselves. I listened to the wisdom and not just to the person. My ability to be faithful has nothing to do with anyone else. So, I will continue to take criticism from people who need to take a look in the mirror themselves. Whatever is hard for you to do, do that!

6. I decided to live my life having faith in God. I had put my faith in a lot of people who let me down and lied to me. Now I put God first, because I have learned it's better to put your trust in God rather than any human. Without faith and hope, people are in trouble. I live my life now expecting great things from God (1 John 3:22).

7. I decided to make new friends. I will never forget where I have come from, and I will never look down on my old friends. However, I had to find new friends to become the man I am today. I have friends today who own businesses. I have friends today who have investments, and we talk about 401ks, stocks and bonds, rental properties, and different streams of income. My new friends can't walk around with their money in their pockets, nor do they want to.

Some of my new friends didn't live the street life, but I still wouldn't advise running up on them. Some of these friends have multiple homes and are quiet givers who don't live a selfish lifestyle. They live for more than just getting high or drunk. They are not trying to impress people with their clothes. These friends and I are investing in others and living with a divine purpose together. For anyone trying to change, I recommend finding some new friends.

In chapter 22, I will give you the last seven of the fourteen keys that changed my life because I chose to believe and decided to live differently. I know the future is bright for the person who decides it's time to change.

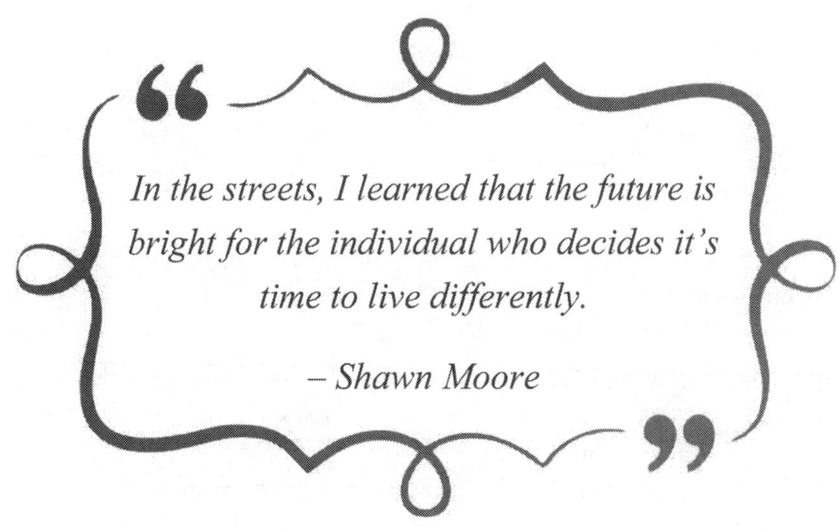

In the streets, I learned that the future is bright for the individual who decides it's time to live differently.

– Shawn Moore

CHAPTER TWENTY TWO

THE FUTURE

If you want to do something different in the future, you must find someone who is doing what you want to do and learn from them and follow in their footsteps. Everything I did, I learned from someone.

8. I decided to start reading at least thirty minutes a day. I tell people if you don't read, that means you are relying on the information you already know, and that leaves no room for growth. Reading enhances our knowledge and vocabulary. Reading helps us avoid communication breakdowns based on gaining new and broader perspectives from different authors. When I first changed, I was reading about four hours a day. Two hours of that time was reading my Bible.

9. I decided to fellowship with like-minded family members. That meant calling my aunts and uncles more, because they were older and had knowledge I could glean from. I don't understand how people just don't care about family like they used to. Family should be important to us. Right now, next to my wife, my parents are my best friends. I have been trying to do a better job myself at reaching out to more of my family members even now at the age of 52 years old.

10. I decided to forgive people. Holding on to grudges will only hinder your progress. Let go of the past. I try to focus on my future, not my past. Have you ever tried to drive with your eyes staring in the rearview mirror? You will not get far at all. The same is true when we choose to hold on to past hurts.

11. I decided to pray more. I have developed a strong prayer life. I talk to God about my past, present, and future. I know that God hears our prayers. However, "His ways are not like our ways" (see Isaiah 55:8–9). So we can't treat God like Santa Claus or a genie. Our prayers should not be selfish, but biblical. I would recommend anyone trying to change to spend at least 15 minutes a day in prayer, and preferably more.

12. I decided to keep working. Lazy people will never be able to change. Change requires hard work and determination. I tell people to find a legitimate job or create one. Do whatever it takes to keep a job until you find a better one.

When you start off, don't worry about the pay. Some money is better than no money or dirty money. Don't despise fast food or retail. At least those who work there are earning an honest living. If you learn how to budget your money, even a few thousand dollars a year can go a long way.

13. I decided to stay actively involved in church. I tell people to find a church that is preaching the gospel of Jesus Christ. In the end, there will be no real change apart from a relationship with God through the person of Jesus Christ. A real man of God will help you in this life and prepare you for the one to come.

There is absolutely nothing wrong with being prosperous and healthy, but we are not staying here. This earth is not our eternal home. People need to find a man of God who teaches doctrine and knows the difference between exegesis and eisegesis—between pulling out what God says and putting into the text the preacher's own ideas. Everyone should keep growing spiritually by being part of a local church.

14. I decided to strive for excellence and live with an attitude of gratitude. How you feel can significantly impact your behavior. If you don't feel good about your life, it's hard to give your best.

When we intentionally choose to be grateful instead of complaining all the time, the sky is the limit. I decided to be not a talker but a doer. I try hard to be a man of my word. I know my reputation will speak louder than my words. Our reputation will open doors for us or close them.

I try my best to respect the opinions of others, but I will never live by them. Don't let what people say about you or what you are going through hinder you from giving your all. Never settle for mediocracy.

In chapter 23 I will share with you what I did at the age of nine that I believe separates my story from others.

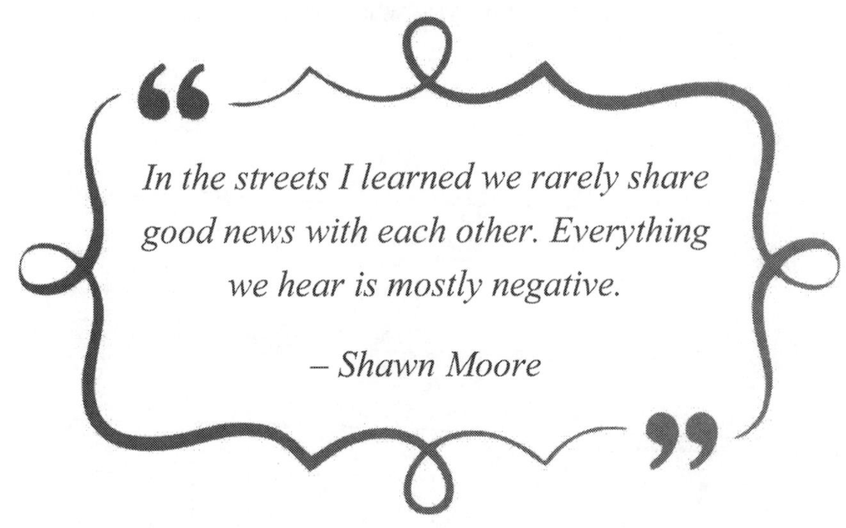
In the streets I learned we rarely share good news with each other. Everything we hear is mostly negative.
– Shawn Moore

CHAPTER TWENTY THREE

NINE

The overall purpose of me sharing my story is to make sure God is venerated as the gracious, merciful, great, loving God that He is. When Shawn Moore tells his story, it is for God to get the glory. I would not be the person I am or doing what I am doing if it wasn't for God.

When I put my faith in the gospel message of Jesus Christ at the age of nine years old. God really did start doing a work in my life. He protected me as only a loving God will. He protected me because of my relationship with Him. You can't disobey God, and not be faithful in church. Then get mad at God for how our life has turned out. Even though I wasn't going to church. I have always lived understanding life was not just about me. I always tried to respect and live like there is a God.

Do you know that life is not all about you? What are you doing right now to honor and bring glory to God?

I almost destroyed my life focusing too much on what people thought about me. Trying to get people to like and accept me almost cost me my life. I'd rather be accepted by God rather than man any day because people are fake, fickle and will switch up on you.

I am so grateful I decided to live focused on the standards of God and not on what people think. People think they can live anyway they want and still have a relationship with God. That's simply not true. Only through God's righteousness can a person be in the right relationship with God.

The Bible teaches about three different kinds of righteousness. Righteousness is the state of being acceptable to God because we have met God's moral standards.

Man has always and will continue to fall short unless they come to God the way God has designed for man to be in relationship with Him (Isaiah 64:6). If we depend on our own righteousness, we must admit we fall short and mess up sometimes so the righteousness of man will not be accepted by God (James 2:10; Galatians 2:16; Romans 10:4; Philippians 3:9).

If we depend on the righteousness that comes from following God's law, once again we must admit that we fall short and disobey God sometimes. So, the righteousness of the law will not be accepted by God. The only righteousness that is accepted by God is that righteousness He gives to those who believe. It is God who saves His people from sin, not we ourselves (2 Corinthians 5:21).

The Bible teaches that God sent His Son Jesus to die for our sins (John 3:16; 1 Corinthians 15:3–4). God wants to forgive you like God forgave me. When I asked Him to help me, that's exactly what He did. He forgave me not because of what I had done, but because of what His Son has done.

God wants you to spend eternity with Him in heaven. When we accept Jesus as our Saviour, relying on Him to deliver us, we become a part of God's family. We must choose Jesus to have a relationship with God.

God is the Father of mercies. His mercy endures forever (see Psalm 118). Through God's mercy, you can have a relationship with God. Yes, we have all sinned and come up short of doing that which pleases God (Romans 3:23). There is no one who is completely innocent (Romans 3:10–18).

Death is a consequence of disobeying God (Genesis 2:15–17; Genesis 3; Genesis 5:5; Romans 6:23). The punishment for sinning or disobeying God is death both physically and spiritually. But through faith in Jesus, we can pass from death into everlasting life with God (John 5:24). This promise is made possible by a loving God (Romans 5:8) who cannot lie (Romans 3:4; Numbers 23:19).

Jesus paid the price for our sins. All we have to do is repent and confess with our mouth Jesus as Lord and believe in our hearts that God raised Him from the dead. When you do this, the Bible declares you will be saved (Romans 10:9).

If you are tired of living your life foolishly, if you want to change your life like I did, all you have to do is give your life to God now (Romans 10:13: "For whoever calls upon the name of the Lord shall be saved.").

All you have to do is do what I did when I was nine years old. I prayed to God and acknowledged I knew I was a sinner. I know I deserved to die. I knew I didn't deserve to be in a relationship with God. But I thanked God for sending Jesus to die and take the punishment that I deserved through faith in Him. I was asking for forgiveness. I trusted only in Jesus for salvation (John 14:6) and have been enjoying with confidence the gift of eternal life from that moment until now.

If you have believed like I did and said a simple prayer to God, the Bible declares you to be saved. Now I challenge you to find a sound church that preaches the gospel of Jesus Christ (I John 5:13–15). Don't stop growing. Remember the only reason my life has turned out the way it did compared to so many others is because I decided to choose Christ at the age of nine. Even though there were many years after I was saved that I didn't obey God, He preserved my life. If you trusted in God many years ago but are not living for Him now, turn back to Him. While it is never too late, it is also unwise to wait. Turn to Him today. If you want to be different or do something different with your life. I am telling you. You Can! You must first decide it's okay to be different. I am not trying to be a Christian but a Christ-follower. A Christ follower is someone who is doing their best to be like Christ without losing who God created them to be. I decided it was ok to be different and from then on I have put in work with God's help to be different. If you want to be different start with deciding to be a Christ follower like me. I decided to follow the example of Jesus. You can ask anyone in prison, jail or still living the street life and they will tell you life doesn't always go as planned. Everyone wants to be successful at something. Setting the goal to emulate rappers or those living the street life is selling ourselves way too short. We need to dream bigger. We need to be willing to use our brains, be patient, and put in the work. Successful people don't allow where they are in life to stop them from dreaming. Successful people understand mistakes and failure is a big part of life. But successful people always focus on what's next. After all the mistakes I made in my life, what's most important is when I decided I needed to change and did something about it. The world we live in is filled with hate but I believe in love. I know where my life would be if I didn't love God and let God love me. Can you look back over your life where God was showing you love but maybe you didn't see it at the time? It's my desire now to let everybody know that God lives in me by how I live and how I show love to everyone like God has loved on me. I believe and know the Future is bright for the individual who decides its time to Change. If you would like to hear Shawn preach the word of God. Look him up at BRBC KCMO youtube page or BRBCKC.org and subscribe.

If this book has blessed you or you have any questions about what you believe, I would love to hear from you at

Shawnmooreministries.com
or
Shawnmooreministries@gmail.com

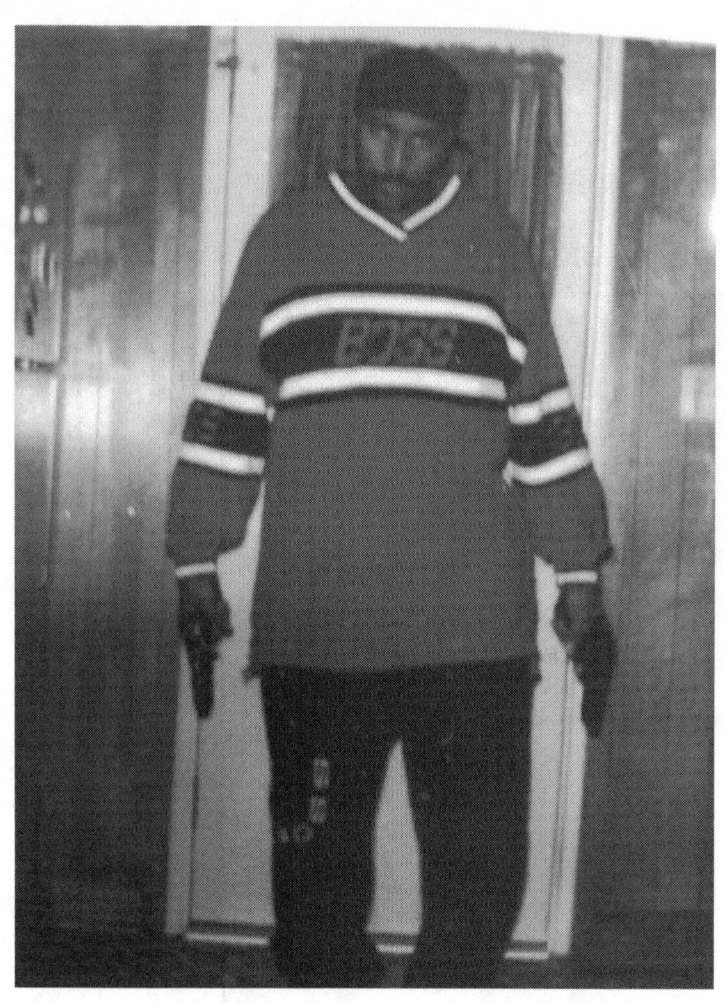
BOSS

"NO MATTER WHERE YOU FIND YOURSELF IN LIFE DON'T FORGET WHERE YOU COME FROM."

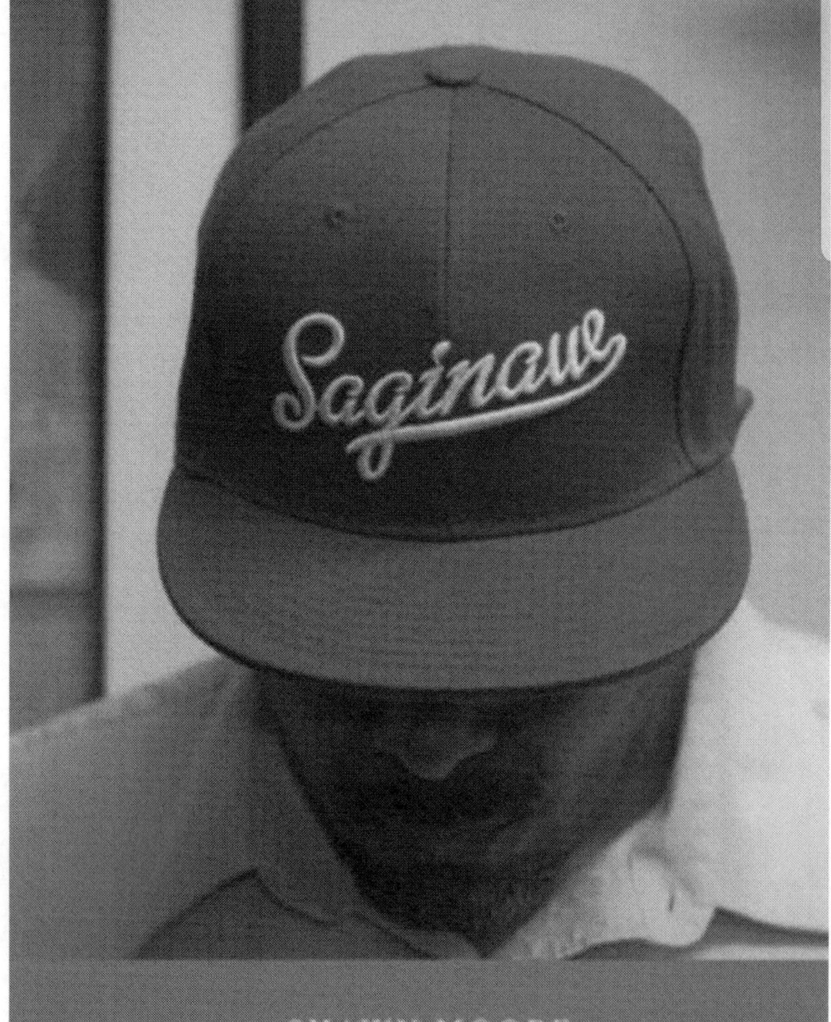

SHAWN MOORE
"CHANGE IS POSSIBLE IF YOU BELIEVE"

Made in the USA
Columbia, SC
15 September 2024

41779065R10076